RESPECTED

How One Word Can Change More
Than Just Your Love Life

By Akirah Robinson

This book is dedicated to my late grandmother, Betsy Wright.

Her spunk, her work ethic, and her desire to serve others were just a few of the reasons why she was respected by so many.

Her life wasn't always easy, though. It took experiencing a period of "darkness" before she realized her worth and left the darkness behind. It's because of her example, however, that I eventually left my "darkness" behind too.

And now, the legacy she leaves behind is full of light.

TABLE OF CONTENTS

INTRODUCTION

If I had my way, every gal in the universe would understand the importance of being respected in her relationships. That includes you. And the gal next to you. And her second cousin.

My entire love life completely changed after I started receiving respect from the men I dated. Not only did I stop attaching myself to unkind men, I somehow stopped attracting them too. I had much more fun with dating because I was no longer rushing to find a husband. Instead, I started spending my precious time with men who treated me the way I deserve. During times when dates were few and far between, I had no problem living my life and creating happiness on my own.

After so many failed attempts at dating, it was as if a light bulb went off and all the pressure I had put on myself to find "The One" suddenly lifted. Being respected became my number one priority. And I think it should be yours too.

I have no clue what your love life looks like right now. You might be happily single, contemplating a breakup, or dating your pretty butt off. No matter what phase of life you're in currently, I want you to know you deserve to be respected.

In fact, I want respect to come so naturally to you that you don't even think about it when you require it. I want you to be the gal who doesn't compromise her standards just because she's tired of being single.

But the important question is: Do you want to be that gal?

If so, keep reading.

***

As a breakup coach (yes, that's a real thing), I help women heal from heartache and learn how to date smarter. I absolutely love my work and I'm always amazed that I have the opportunity to connect with such wonderful women all over the world.

While I think I'm great at what I do, I know I'm not the best coach for every woman I meet. You see, even though I write a lot about love and dating, I don't claim to be a dating connoisseur. In fact, dating experts kind of perplex me.

About ten years ago, I desperately wanted to get married. I read so many books about dating that it almost didn't make sense how I could still be single. I followed each rule given to me religiously. I never called or texted men first because I didn't want to seem too eager. I dated multiple men at once so that I wouldn't get too attached to any of them. I also maintained my appearance by buying new clothes each month, exercising regularly, and getting my nails done every Saturday.

Doing those things in and of themselves was not unhealthy, but I was overly meticulous about everything I did, in hopes of finding my husband. My desire for marriage was unhealthy because I was dating from a place of utter desperation. I'm almost certain the men I dated could sense this, which is probably why I struggled to find a healthy and stable relationship.

It took a while, but eventually I realized that relationships are non-formulaic, especially romantic ones. There's no guarantee that implementing a set of dating rules can ensure we'll meet the right person and live happily ever after. I'm afraid that in our society, which glorifies immediate gratification and certainty, we sometimes fail to accept that. I definitely fell into this trap.

Life is a mysterious mix of beautiful, challenging, and painful experiences. No one can predict how it will unfold and we don't always understand why it unfolds the way it does. There's no dating book or relationship expert in the world who can tell you exactly what to do in order to find love. Certainly there are situations where meeting someone and falling in love are possible, but really, there are no step-by-step instructions for any of this. I mean, if there was, we'd all be married with 2.5 kids, right?

This is why I don't promise any client that I can help her find the love of her life…unless she's willing to call herself the love of her life. When I work with women, I don't view their single lives as big messes to be fixed. I don't believe they're single because they aren't happy enough on their own or they need to go back to therapy or they need to lose some more weight. Not only do those explanations seem like the wrong answers, but asking "Why am I still single?" feels like the wrong question.

Instead, I work best with women who are ready to put themselves first. These women understand that doing the hard work of healing, facing their issues, and creating the lives they want to live right now will better prepare them to participate in a healthy relationship in the future. Doing those things will also help them thrive as they wait patiently for their Someone Special.

If you're blessed with something before you're ready to fully enjoy and handle it, it can quickly turn into a burden. And neither one of us wants that to happen. Hence, this book.

Respected is divided into three sections. In the first section, we will explore the necessity of loving ourselves before we try to love someone else (or ask someone else to love us). The second section contains my best advice on how to expect respect within romantic relationships and uphold the standards that match our deepest desires. I also discuss how to move forward after a difficult breakup (I wouldn't be a breakup coach if I didn't talk about breakups in my first book, right?). The last section is filled with stories of heartache from some of the most wonderful women I know. I think it's quite likely that you will find their stories as inspirational as I do, as each one of these women has learned what it means to be respected and to flourish in the midst of hardship.

Additionally, at the end of each chapter, you will find questions for you to consider. I suggest answering these questions in your journal, or finding a close friend with whom you can discuss the answers.

The pages ahead will dig deep into the topic of respect, and how it truly can change more than just your love life. But before we get into all of that, here's a little more of my story and my struggles with expecting respect, particularly throughout an abusive relationship I was in during my early twenties.

***

I used to be what some people would call a late bloomer. I never dated in high school. In fact, I didn't have my first real kiss until I was twenty-one years old. While my peers were swapping spit, I was busy doing homework and going to youth group. No boys for me.

That's not to say I wasn't interested. I wouldn't have minded having a boyfriend in high school—it's just that no one ever showed interest. I had loads of friends, male and female, but never any dating prospects. As one of the only black girls in my school, many of my male friends seemed more interested in dating my white peers. And weighing in at almost 225 pounds, I had low self-esteem, too.

This gave me plenty of time to daydream about the "perfect boyfriend". A rugged, brown-eyed, guitar-playing dreamboat is what my heart really wanted, or so I thought at the time. Every night I would pray for God to send him to me soon.

But as I said, no one came along until I was twenty-one. By then, I had lost seventy pounds and felt a lot less patient. I wanted a boyfriend...yesterday. I found myself becoming less and less picky as time went on.

For example, when I was in high school, I attended church on a regular basis. I fantasized about a boyfriend who would go to church with me, pray with me, and share my faith. Yet when an atheist asked me out on a date years later, I immediately agreed. It seemed like everyone else was dating and I wanted to too. I was very tired of being single.

Not going to church with me was the least of my worries though, because this guy wasn't very nice to me. He never called when he said he would and he frequently stood me up to hang out with his friends. I thought having a boyfriend would make me feel better about myself, but with him, I just felt crappy. It was clear that he only wanted to see me when it was convenient for him. I worked hard to earn his attention, with very little success. It felt terrible trying to convince my "boyfriend" to care about me.

That still didn't stop me from seeing him. Like I said, I was tired of being single. It wasn't until I randomly met someone else who was interested in me that I felt ready to break it off. Yes, my first boyfriend was pretty mad, but I felt little guilt. My new boyfriend treated me like a queen.

This new man wooed me in a way I had never experienced before. He made me feel special by buying me flowers and taking me on fancy dates. For the first time in my life, I felt beautiful! I fell in love hard, and I fell in love fast. Quickly, I began planning our wedding and naming our babies.

Respected

As time progressed, however, I started to see other sides of him.

I soon learned that he didn't like me talking to other guys. Just mentioning another man's name in conversation was enough to start an argument. He didn't even want me to be Facebook friends with them. It seemed odd, but in order to keep the peace, I spent one Saturday afternoon unfriending every man I was connected to on Facebook. Instantly I felt regret, especially since it didn't really solve anything. He continued to give me grief every time I interacted with other men at work and school. It seemed that nothing I did was ever good enough for him.

He was never very friendly to my friends either, even when I begged him to be nice. Instead, he'd accuse me of cheating on him when I spent time with them. One time he sent my best friend hateful messages on Facebook because she took me to see a concert one night and we stayed out later than he thought we should have. His childish behavior was incredibly embarrassing, but since I didn't know what to do, I avoided this friend for quite some time afterward.

If I didn't answer his phone calls immediately, he would continue to call me until I did. Other times, he would look through the text messages on my phone behind my back. Clearly he did not trust me, but rather than taking responsibility for this, he blamed an ex-girlfriend who cheated on him. Thinking I could make up for her mistakes, I did all I could to reassure him that I would never be unfaithful. In hindsight, it's not surprising that my attempts did not satisfy him.

When he got really angry, things would get physical. He would push me against a wall, yell at me, and call me names. During our most heated arguments, he'd even attempt to strangle me. Physical violence wasn't a frequent occurrence between us, so each time he apologized, I forgave him. I knew relationships require a lot of effort and I wanted to do whatever it took to make ours successful. Unfortunately it felt like I was doing most of the work.

It took a terrifying incident of violence one December evening to finally convince me to leave. This decision, the best one of my life, was the start of a long healing process. I cannot even begin to describe the pain and hope I simultaneously experienced as I slowly started to make my well-being, not his, a priority.

***

You might be wondering why it took me four long years to finally break up with him. Sometimes, I wonder that, too. Five years after ending that relationship, I still struggle to understand why I was so stuck on making it work. Honestly, I think it was a combination of things.

First, I loved him. This man knew how to push my buttons, but he also knew how to make me smile. I know it sounds odd, but our relationship wasn't all bad. We shared many special moments together and in spite of his efforts to control me, I often felt protected by him.

Second, I was terrified of being single. During my early to mid-twenties, many of my girlfriends were getting engaged, and I hated the thought of being left out. I mean, it took me twenty-one years to find a boyfriend—who knew when I'd find another?! Being single again was completely unappealing and despite the many positive and loving people in my life, I equated singleness with being alone. Not wanting to experience the loneliness that haunted me from my teenage years, I held on to my ex-boyfriend for dear life.

Third, I knew breaking up with him would hurt and I wanted to put off dealing with the pain for as long as I could. It's true that breakups can be very painful, and mine was no exception. Unfortunately, I had no idea how eye-opening and life-changing breakups can be as well. I never realized that I was stunting my emotional and developmental growth by staying in an unhealthy relationship for so long. It wasn't until I was out of the relationship that I ran a 10K, started graduate school, earned a promotion at work, lived in my first apartment on my own, and traveled across the country by myself. I did all of these things within my first year of being single again. Slowly, I began to understand how stifling my toxic relationship actually was. Only after leaving him did space in my life open up for me to grow and experience new things.

Fourth, I didn't even know that my ex-boyfriend's behaviors were classified as abuse. Surely there were things about him that upset me, but I just chalked them up to my inexperience with relationships. When he told me to stop talking to other men or asked me to end certain friendships, I figured these were normal requests and things I needed to do in order to be a good girlfriend. No one ever taught me the warning signs of abuse, so I didn't know that partner abuse is about power and control, and therefore can take more forms than just physical violence. Unfortunately, by the time my ex-boyfriend began hurting me physically, I felt too embarrassed to seek help.

Lastly, I naïvely thought I could change him. I believed that if I just held out a little longer, took him to therapy, found him a new job, and managed all of his money, he would slowly grow up and become the man I wanted him to be. Regardless of my intentions, it took a while for me to realize that wanting to change him was just as controlling as him wanting to change me. I fell in love with his potential, making it very difficult to accept reality as it actually was. This fact definitely added to the anxiety I felt when I thought about leaving him.

Years later, leaving my abusive relationship remains one of the hardest things I've ever done. It destroyed me to make such a painful decision and for many weeks I believed my life was beyond repair. I invested a lot of time and energy into our relationship and felt like an absolute failure for letting it all go. Eventually, I began to see that breaking up with my ex-boyfriend granted me the life-changing opportunity to completely recreate myself.

Many tears and failed dating attempts later, I did recreate myself. More specifically, I fell in love with myself. Abuse changed me, but it didn't define me. And now I can tell you with 100% confidence that your relationship history (or lack thereof) doesn't have to define you either.

* * *

It's not my fault my ex-boyfriend abused me. Sure, I stayed with him a little longer than I should have, but that doesn't mean I deserved to be treated badly. As a grown man, he knew the difference between right and wrong. In some circumstances, he chose to be wrong by doing hurtful things. Other times, he chose to be awesome. Either way, I can't be blamed for any of his actions.

I say this because if you are being treated badly in a relationship, you need to know it is NOT your fault. You might feel like it is, but it isn't.

Perhaps you are confused. Maybe it doesn't feel safe to leave. Maybe the thought of starting all over scares the crap out of you. I share my story because if there is any portion of it that resonates with yours, it's important that you know you are not alone.

Take your time. Seek support if you safely can (I've listed a handful of resources at the end of this book that you may find helpful). I imagine you're asking yourself some difficult questions. As you search for the answers, rely on the caring folks who are in your corner and will give you the space you need to find them.

Never let anyone convince you that you're the reason for someone else's actions.

You're not. You're wonderful. And you deserve to be treated as such.

You deserve to be respected.

PART 1: LOVE YOURSELF

JUST IMAGINE

"Everything you can imagine is real."

-Pablo Picasso

Take a few deep breaths. Clear your mind. Find a relaxing position for your body and then imagine the following scenarios:

What if you never let yourself heal from the heartache? What if you keep dating people who make you feel bad about yourself? What if you continue to use food, sex, relationships, alcohol, or drugs to distract yourself from reality? What if you keep comparing your life to others'? What if every time you see yourself naked, you only point out the flaws and not the beauty? What if you keep settling? What if you continue to doubt? What if you marry the wrong person, even though you know you shouldn't?

What if you never learn to love yourself?

I don't know about you, but none of those scenarios sound very fun to me. In fact, they sound downright exhausting, frustrating, and painful. I know because many of those scenarios were a reality for much of my life, until I realized that they didn't have to be. At that

Respected

point, I started to see how much I had been settling throughout my life. Perhaps you can relate.

But what would happen if you decided that you no longer want any of the above scenarios to be your reality? What if you decided that regularly numbing yourself, hating yourself, or not letting yourself heal were no longer acceptable ways to live? What if you decided, today, that enough is enough? How might your life look different?

Listen: You are your responsibility. And I'm not talking about getting to work on time or making sure you have enough clean underwear for the week (although those things are very important). What I mean is, it's up to you to make sure you are not a basket case. Many of your issues don't have to grip you in fear or consume your mind all the livelong day. No, they won't magically disappear, but your life can be so much more than your areas of struggle, if you want it to be.

I'm not promising you a life free of challenges or saying that you'll easily be able to do this on your own. I do believe, however, that you are fully capable of living the life you truly want to live. How? By taking care of yourself and listening to yourself. By trusting yourself and every once in a while, asking for help when you need it.

There are no guarantees that anyone else is going to let you off the hook by doing those things for you. But I have a feeling you're not the type of gal who wants to be let off the hook. Something tells me that if you're reading a book like this one, you're willing to do the work it takes to live your life to the fullest. The first section of this book is about just that.

Questions to consider:

A year from now, what do you want your life to look like?

What do you have to do now in order to make your vision a reality later?

SELF-WORTH IS THE FOUNDATION

"Worthiness doesn't have prerequisites."

–Brene Brown

WORTH *(noun)* **1.** A quality that commands esteem or respect; merit.

You have so much of that, my friend. Do you know that?

I really hope so. And if you don't, I hope you will by the end of this book. Because when you know that you're worthy, something inside of you changes. It feels good to grow into your new confidence; scary at times, but good. What you settled for in the past just doesn't fly anymore. Suddenly, life becomes a glorious adventure instead of an 80-year-long source of stress.

That doesn't mean you will never struggle. Society does a great job at making us doubt our worth.

But society likes to tell lies. All the stinkin' time.

So chew on this, especially when you're feeling some doubt:

Your worth is not determined by whether or not you are the apple of someone else's eye. It does not depend on whether you are dating someone or are married. It does not depend on what pants size you wear or whether or not you decided to put on lip gloss this morning. And contrary to what you might believe, your worth has absolutely nothing to do with your accomplishments either. Acing your exams or receiving a stellar evaluation at work is fine and dandy, but you're still worthy even when you fail.

To believe otherwise is to believe a dangerous lie.

You came into this world with immense worth—intrinsic worth that cannot be taken away from you. It doesn't matter what your relationship status is, what the scale says, or how much debt you're in. Your worth is in you...your worth IS you.

The sooner you realize that, the better off you'll be. As Marianne Williamson says in her book, *A Woman's Worth*:

"We don't have to do anything to be glorious; to be so is our nature. If we have read, studied, and loved; if we have thought as deeply as we could and felt as deeply as we could; if our bodies are instruments of love given and received—then we are the greatest blessing in the world. Nothing needs to be added to that to establish our worth."

Think of your closest friend. You probably think of her as one of the greatest blessings in your world. Have you ever thought she would be more worthy if she lost ten pounds or got an awesome promotion at work? Of course not! More than likely, you judge your friends based on who they are as individuals and who they are on the inside. In fact, you're probably more inclined to believe that it is because of your friends' worth that they are able to accomplish such wonderful things, not the other way around. You don't love your friends based on what they have; you love them for who they are.

So why do we struggle so hard to approach ourselves in the same way?

I like to think of self-worth as the foundation in our lives. When a builder constructs a house, extra consideration must be taken to ensure that the foundation is sound and secure. There's no way a construction crew would build on top of a shaky foundation because they know the house would quickly topple over at the first sight of bad weather. If that were to happen, it would require much more time and money to repair the damage than if the foundation were constructed correctly in the first place.

I believe our lives are pretty similar. Trying to find the love of your life without first believing you are worthy is like building a home on top of a shaky foundation. Without a deep sense of your own worthiness, you'll likely be looking outside of yourself for completion, validation, and love. This is a blueprint for disaster, for more reasons than one. Rejection, breakups, and long bouts of singleness can easily turn into hurricanes, causing your life, your house, to fall apart.

Sometimes we forget that because pain in life is inevitable, experiences such as rejection and breakups are normal. Having a firm foundation, however, will ensure that when those things do happen (because they will) you'll still have your self-worth to rely on as you cope with the pain and move forward.

Don't spend your life trying to avoid the hard stuff. And don't think for a second that a relationship outside of yourself will fix the hard stuff. Only a loving and healthy relationship with yourself, rooted in a deep sense of self-worth, can help you stand your ground when life's trials arise. It's true that trusting in your own self-worth probably isn't going to happen overnight. Loving ourselves is a lifelong journey, with many twists, turns, bumps, bends, ups, and downs. You won't always feel like loving yourself and some days you will doubt that you're worthy of love and acceptance. There will always be things you won't like about yourself and circumstances in your life that will set you back. These things can be major distractions, if you let them.

But here's the deal:

Regardless of how of how you feel about yourself on any given day, you can commit to deepening your sense of self-worth.

How? By reminding yourself of the truth. Here's a simple trick to help you:

The "But" Trick

Sometimes we get so clouded by our own negativity that we need to take a time-out.

You know what I mean. You step on the scale and feel like a failure for the rest of the day. The guy never calls, even though he said he would. Your Facebook News Feed is filled with wedding photos.

When our lives look different than what we'd like, it's easy to take the blame. Instead of being kind to ourselves during a difficult time, we become bitter, negative, and downright mean. We treat ourselves poorly and wonder why we can't get out of the funk.

It takes time to break the habit of negative self-talk. If you've been talking down to yourself for years, decades even, negativity has probably become a natural response for you. I certainly don't expect you to change this overnight; that's not even reasonable. The "But Trick", on the other hand, is reasonable. It's a tool you can use whenever you need it.

How It Works:

"I hate that I'm single right now. **But I'm still worthy.**"

"I can't believe I gained five pounds. **But I'm still worthy.**"

"Another friend is pregnant?? It feels like it will never be my turn. **But I'm still worthy.**"

"Being unemployed makes me feel like a failure. **But I'm still worthy.**"

"He hasn't texted me back and it's been two days. I feel so rejected. **But I'm still worthy.**"

Sometimes we don't realize that our thoughts only have as much power as we give them. Millions of thoughts pop into our head each day, some positive and some negative. Whether we know it or not, we are constantly choosing which thoughts we give our attention to. If you're a pessimist, like me, you're probably more likely to focus on what's going wrong in your life, rather than what's going right.

You might even feel tempted to accept your negative thoughts as the ultimate truth, rather than challenging them from time to time. But just because a thought enters your mind doesn't mean you have to buy into it. Rather than believing every negative thought that pops into your mind, you can instead view those moments as opportunities to remind yourself of your worth as a human being. In other words, you can choose to respond however you'd like.

Now, I'm not telling you to just put on a happy face when you're feeling crummy. It would be insensitive to ask you to force yourself to feel positively about the upsetting situations in your life. Instead, allow yourself to feel and accept difficult emotions like rejection, pain, dissatisfaction, and jealousy, since they're all a part of the human experience and should not be ignored. Those feelings, however, are no indication of your worth. And there's no need to place permanent judgments on yourself because of temporary emotions.

Besides, has talking down to yourself ever helped you become more successful? Has hating yourself helped you lose any weight (and keep it off)? Does pointing out your flaws actually help you fix them and experience more happiness?

If I had to guess, I'd say the answer to all three of these questions is a big, fat "no!" Because if hating ourselves was truly productive, everyone would be a CEO, diets would actually work, and Beyoncé wouldn't be the only person around town singing the words to "Flawless."

Negative self-talk is simply not effective. At least, not in a sustainable way.

So anytime you catch yourself falling down the rabbit hole of negativity, remember you can stop yourself with the "But Trick". State this mantra (out loud if you need to) that you're still worthy, whether life is going as you'd like it to or not. It may sound incredibly nuts, but trust me, the repetition really helps.

If you want to believe the truth about yourself, you eventually will. It may take some time, but the truth always prevails.

And the truth is this: you're worthy of acceptance, kindness, and love all the same.

Questions to consider:

What negative thoughts are you most susceptible to believing about yourself?

In what ways can you challenge those thoughts and focus more on your intrinsic self-worth instead?

SELF-ISH PRACTICES TO ADOPT

"I think I'll treat myself to all the pretty places in my head." –Stevie Wonder

If self-worth is the foundation, the way we treat ourselves is the frame. Walls set boundaries, right? Well, engaging in regular self-care, self-soothing, and self-awareness communicates to ourselves and to the world what treatment we believe we deserve. Those practices set boundaries and also help us develop deep and meaningful relationships with ourselves.

Unfortunately, however, we sometimes get into the bad habit of asking other people to meet all of our relationship needs, even when we're perfectly capable of meeting many of those needs on our own. Other times, we want people to treat us better than we are willing to treat ourselves. This can cause us some major problems, especially in our relationships. Here's an example from my own life:

There was a time during my marriage that I thought my husband was obligated to be there for me whenever I "needed" him to be. If I thought I looked fat one day, it was his job to tell me I wasn't. If I had a bad day at work, it was his responsibility to give me his undivided attention while I vented.

Wanting to be a good spouse, my poor husband did all he could to meet these demands. About halfway into the first year of our marriage, however, he was starting to lose steam. He vowed to be my husband, not my everything. Even though I knew this, I was being lazy. My neediness was exhausting him, and it wasn't fair. It was time to put on my big girl underpants and start taking care of myself.

Now, I'm not saying you should never look to your loved ones for support and guidance, especially during times of need. I love being there for my friends, and I know I can count on them to be there for me, too. That's what loved ones are for.

On the other hand, if you find yourself reaching out to your friends for constant reassurance and care, I urge you to take a step back and take a good look at your behaviors. Are your actions deepening your relationships or straining them? If you're not careful, you could be at risk of exhausting your loved ones by expecting too much from them. Additionally, it's important for you to learn how to cultivate a healthy relationship with yourself. You'll never learn how if you don't practice, right?

Respected

That said, here are a few good ways you can start being more "self-ish" and foster the positive feelings you want to experience in your life:

Practice self-kindness: If the words "fat", "stupid", or "ugly" come to mind when referring to yourself, then, Houston, we have a problem. So often we don't dare speak to other people the way we speak to ourselves. I think that's a darn shame.

Being nice to yourself doesn't mean you're letting yourself off the hook for your shortcomings, by the way. It just means that you're choosing to give equal weight to your strengths as you do your weaknesses. As Louise Hay once said, "You've been criticizing yourself for years and it hasn't worked. Try approving of yourself and see what happens."

Engage in regular self-care: About a year ago, I confided in a friend that my depression was so overwhelming that I was forgetting to shower on a regular basis. Gross, huh? Rather than judging me, this friend looked me straight in the eyes with such kindness and said, "Akirah, you need to take care of yourself. You deserve a shower."

Immediately, I went home and started to list things I enjoy doing that make me feel cared for. It should not surprise you that "showering" topped the list. When I was finished, I bought some body wash and made it a point to start doing those things.

Learn how to self-soothe: Bad day at work? Failed an exam? Instead of rushing to the nearest person to vent, spend some time alone first.

When in distress, women tend to run to others for validation, support, or advice. For many of us, this can be a hard habit to break. The next time you're feeling stressed, try giving yourself a big bear hug, taking a bubble bath, lighting some candles, or doing a breathing exercise. See if you can calm yourself down a bit before frantically rushing to a friend and adding a bunch of your stress to her day. If you do, chances are your conversation with her will be a lot more productive.

Increase your self-awareness: What makes you smile? What makes you tick? What do you want most in life? How do you want to feel?

If you can't answer those questions, perhaps you should put dating on hold until you can. Would you want to date a person who is confused about who they are? Probably not. Assume that your future spouse feels the same way and take the time you need to truly get to know yourself.

Don't forget self-compassion: Hours just before the clock struck midnight last New Year's Eve, I first learned about self-compassion: the idea that as humans we are worthy of treating ourselves with kindness, particularly when life is painful, difficult, or we're experiencing failure. During those times, rather than talking down to ourselves, it is more effective to comfort ourselves in the same way we would a close friend or family member experiencing hardship.

Immediately I decided that I wanted to learn more about self-compassion and found a book called *Self-Compassion: The Proven Power of Being Kind to Yourself* by Dr. Kristin Neff. I read it cover to cover, and a few months later, read it a second time. I recommend it to any struggling or recovering perfectionist, like myself, who is looking to be nicer to herself in the midst of suffering.

Wrap it all up inside of self-love: Want to know the best news of all? There's no need to wait on someone else to experience a life full of love. Contrary to popular belief, you can create a life brimming with love right now and feel the same way about yourself that you hope someone else will someday.

Your job, if you choose to accept it, is to love and accept yourself as much as you possibly can in this very moment. No if's, and's, or but's, my friend. You are worthy of unconditional love. Especially from your-self.

Question to consider:

How can you apply each of the above self-ish practices into your own life?

A LITTLE MORE ABOUT SELF-CARE

"You'll never feel happy, until you try." -C2C

These days, it seems kind of trendy to talk about self-care, but that doesn't stop me from being obsessed with it. After getting into the habit of regularly practicing self-care, I can't help but adamantly preach its benefits to all my loved ones. Self-care works, my friends. In fact, it's probably my favorite self-ish practice. I've seen the positive effects of it, and now, I'm a believer!

Many times when people think about self-care, they think about getting a pedicure while drinking a glass of wine or watching *Scandal* and eating a pint of Ben & Jerry's. While those things are fun for many people, including myself, it's important to know the difference between pleasurable self-care and nurturing self-care.

Pleasurable self-care is about enjoyment, satisfaction, and comfort. As humans, we're wired to gravitate towards these things because they feel good. If you're not careful, however, pleasure can soon turn into a vice to distract you from your real life. Why else do you think Facebook is so addicting?

Some examples of pleasurable self-care: Getting a pedicure, channel surfing, napping, etc.

Nurturing self-care, on the other hand, is all about you being your true authentic self. When you are engaging in nurturing self-care, you are reminding yourself of what makes you unique and what makes you feel alive. Nurturing self-care may require a little more effort than pleasurable self-care, but it's incredibly important that you incorporate this type of care into your life when you can.

Some examples of nurturing self-care: Going to a yoga class, taking a hike, reading a book, journaling, and the like.

So how exactly do you determine whether you should take part in acts of pleasurable self-care or nurturing self-care? I think that question is best answered by asking another: "What does my soul and body NEED right now?" If you think you need to veg out a bit and relax, choose a pleasurable activity to help you unwind. When you're looking to feel alive and regain some confidence, choose a nurturing self-care activity instead.

And be honest with yourself. Yes, it takes more energy to go to a yoga class than to sit on the couch and eat Ben & Jerry's, but if your body needs yoga, don't deny your body yoga! Remember, one type of care is not better than the other. We need both pleasure and nurturing in order to lead balanced lives.

Self-care also consists of making decisions on how to spend your time and with whom you spend it. Perhaps you're feeling incredibly exhausted and need to decline an invitation to a party. Or maybe a personal day off from work is exactly what you need to feel grounded again. Give yourself permission to make decisions that will set healthy boundaries for yourself and help you safeguard your well-being.

Despite how it may initially sound, self-care and the other self-ish activities are not actually about being selfish at the expense of other people. I'm not encouraging you to call off work on a day your co-workers really need you, or to miss your best friend's birthday party because you can't stand some of her other friends. When caring for ourselves, we must remember to be respectful while ensuring that our needs are met. No, you can't always please everyone—but don't let that stop you from being gracious to others, even when your self-care may cause them a bit of disappointment.

Additionally, adopting a regular self-care routine will not only alleviate your stress and contribute to your well-being, but will also help you strengthen a loving relationship with yourself before you get into a serious relationship. Although our relationships with ourselves are the most important ones we have, they often fall to the wayside when we start dating someone new. It's normal for couples to isolate themselves from the world when they first meet, which is why it's crucial to get into the habit of taking care of yourself before meeting your Someone Special. That way, you'll be much more likely to do so after you meet.

The bottom line is that setting good boundaries for yourself by engaging in self-care on a regular basis is super important. Back when depression hit me like a truck, my own well-being was not a priority and I had no self-care routine to fall back on. I'm not saying self-care alone would have cured my depression; I barely had the energy to shower, remember? But I soon learned that a combination of therapy, anti-depressants, support from my loved ones, and self-care was exactly what I needed to cope with my sadness.

How I Started Taking Care of Myself

After my friend told me I deserved regular showers and I made a list of my most-loved activities, I decided I needed more accountability. Feeling crafty, I whipped out a piece of construction paper and cut out a big heart. On it, I wrote down all of the activities from my list, along with a few others.

After admiring my work for a bit, I knew my heart needed to be displayed in a prominent place. My depression meant I was feeling pretty lethargic and spending most of my time on the couch, in sweats, pouting. I decided to tape my heart on the wall next to the couch and promised myself that each day thereafter I would do at least one activity on my heart, in addition to showering and praying. I told my husband about my Self-Care Heart and asked him to encourage me to follow through on my promise.

These days, I still do at least one activity from my heart every single day. In fact, I cannot even think about starting my day without showering and praying. I've gotten into a decent habit of caring for myself daily, even if I can only commit to fifteen minutes to do so. I've found that spending time alone doing things that make my soul feel alive has helped me fall deeper in love with myself and my life. I'm also less desperate for others to care for me because I've learned ways to cope on my own.

I recognize that my schedule allows for me to make my well-being a priority, largely because I do not yet have children. Additionally, I am grateful to have enough resources to do things I enjoy doing. If you have a grueling work schedule, a few children, or lots of homework to do, engaging in self-care every day may seem like a daunting task. A Self-Care Heart might sound incredibly cheesy, so if it doesn't work for you, try something else that does.

What's most important is that you get into the habit of caring for yourself, however that best works for your life. If that means making a list of activities you really enjoy and choosing one when you're feeling a little run-down, then great! Other people, however, need a little more consistency in their self-care routines. Here are five other ways to work self-care into your schedule on a regular basis:

1. If you're pressed for time, try waking up fifteen minutes earlier a few times a week. Nothing beats starting your day in a calm and peaceful way. Meditating, doing a few yoga poses, reading the newspaper, or fixing yourself a healthy breakfast won't take too much time out of your schedule, but are all great ways to show yourself care and consideration.

2. Find a self-care buddy and set up regular dates with her. Instead of focusing your time on solely pleasurable activities, be intentional about engaging in nurturing self-care together as well.

3. Create a nighttime routine that makes you feel wonderful. Loneliness strikes hard for many people in the evening, which makes it the perfect time to give yourself extra comfort. This might mean lighting a

candle, sending a close friend a goodnight text, journaling about what was great about your day, or watching a show you really enjoy. When I lived alone, I loved eating a caramel crunch rice cake while watching *Chelsea Lately* in bed. Shortly after adopting this routine, I began looking forward to my nights alone.

4. Each month, pick one day to do something spectacular for yourself. Planning something special every month will give you something to look forward to (and might make it easier for all you moms to make childcare plans ahead of time).

5. If you're completely pressed for time, incorporate self-care into your already set schedule. Rock out to your favorite CD during your commute home or sit outside with your journal during your lunch break. The key task for this option is to savor the self-care as much as possible in the moment. Mentally, you must find a way to separate yourself from everyday life, set other tasks aside, and truly put your well-being first, even if only for fifteen minutes.

Hopefully these few ideas will get you thinking about how you can add more self-care into your routine. Feel free to tweak any of these suggestions, as you see fit. Ultimately, it is up to you to decide what will work best for your life. It may take a bit for you to work out the kinks, but I believe it's possible for you to care for yourself on a consistent basis.

You deserve pleasure and you deserve to be nurtured. When you make sure you get both on the regular, you're respecting yourself. And when you show respect towards yourself, you'll be more likely to expect it from others.

And we all know how I feel about that.

So let the self-care begin!

Questions to consider:

What are your five favorite pleasurable self-care activities?

What are your five favorite nurturing self-care activities?

 How will you incorporate more of both into your schedule?

10 WAYS TO SHOW YOURSELF THAT YOU CARE

"Love is the great miracle cure. Loving ourselves works miracles in our lives." –Louise Hay

Need more ideas of what you can add to your own Self-Care Heart? I asked my Facebook followers how they like to remind themselves that they're worthy. Here's what they said:

Solo Date Night: What's most empowering about taking yourself out on a date is that you can do so on your terms. No one else's schedule or preferences really matter when you're planning the night of your life. You can explore your city, see a movie, or try a new restaurant.

If this sounds scary, start small. Instead of buying yourself a three-course dinner, savor a latte at Starbucks. You can even buy yourself flowers first. Romance isn't just for couples, you know.

Taking yourself out on a date is a great way to engage in self-care. Pick something you really enjoy doing and go do it. You just might enjoy your own company more than you think.

Body Part Heart-to-Heart: Is there a part of your body that you've put through the ringer? The two of you might need to have a heart-to-heart. I've never been a fan of my tummy or my thighs. To be quite honest, for twenty-nine years, they've been two of my biggest enemies. After coming to this realization, I've decided to incorporate body part heart-to-hearts into my regular self-care routine. During these chats, I apologize to my body for my self-deprecating remarks and thank it for all it does for me. Afterward, I usually feel more at peace and in awe of my body's strength. Try having a body part heart-to-heart and see if it helps you feel more at peace with your body too.

Write Down 100 Things You Like About Yourself: Yeah, that's right. 100 things.

It probably won't be the easiest thing you've ever done, but you can do it. Just take as much time as you need to complete it and have fun. It doesn't matter if it takes you a week, a month, or even a year to finish it. When it's done, you'll be able to read your list on days when you're feeling a little down on yourself.

Invest In Yourself: In the aftermath of breaking up with my ex, I decided to invest in my life by going to counseling every other week. After sacrificing so much of myself for four years, it felt a little weird to regularly dump all of my troubles onto someone else. It took a few weeks for me to realize how much I deserved and needed to take care of myself in this way. My counselor helped me dig deep into some major issues and understand myself differently. This, in turn, empowered me to live differently as well.

Investing in yourself can be as simple as getting a pedicure or as big as enrolling in a new school program. When we decide to invest in ourselves, we show ourselves and others that we believe we are worth the time, money, and effort it takes for the investment to come to fruition. If you're yearning for a change in your life, I urge you to find a way to invest in yourself. Then, see how you grow as a result.

Move Your Body: I'm not going to tell you to work out three times a week for sixty minutes. I won't tell you to do yoga and go running and lift weights, either. Those suggestions can all be good things to do, but certainly not necessary. What's most important is that you learn how you enjoy moving your body and for you to engage in those activities as much as you can. Hiking, dancing, or hula-hooping all seem like good options, so if you like them, do those things. As Elle Woods says, exercise gives you endorphins, and endorphins make you happy.

So move your body and be happy.

Get Some Rest: Sometimes the most loving thing we can do for ourselves is to take a break; to rest, recharge, and regroup. If you're feeling overwhelmed, uncertain, and confused, you might benefit from a nap or three. Get into the habit of designating a whole day each week for rest and only rest. Doing so will not only get you into the practice of loving yourself, but it will teach you to show appreciation for your precious time and energy as well.

Eat Something That Tastes Heavenly: Show love towards those taste buds of yours and allow them to enjoy a heavenly dish. You get bonus points if you make it yourself with some real quality ingredients, but if you have a history of starting kitchen fires (like me), you can find someone else to make it for you.

(McDonald's doesn't count, though. Neither does Subway. Even Jared deserves a heavenly treat from time to time. You do, too.)

Start a Gratitude Practice: Did you know that expressing gratitude correlates positively with happiness? It does! After learning this, a good friend and I shared one thing we felt grateful for with one another, each day for one month. Not only did I feel closer to my friend, but I felt more appreciative of my life. If you haven't already, I encourage you to adopt a gratitude practice of your own. You can do it with a friend, download the Happier app, or write a short journal entry every night before bed. There are so many things to be grateful for in life, but unfortunately we often lose sight of the small things like tasty food, warm sunshine, or catching the bus just in time. Try practicing gratitude on a regular basis and take notice of how your mindset shifts.

Beautify To Stay Super Fly: I'll be the first to admit that I struggle with this one. (What can I say? I love my sweatpants!) There are days, however, when I have a strong desire to feel pretty. On these days, I'll paint my nails, wear some heels, or do something new with my hair. I've found that these simple things can make a world of a difference in my day...or even my week. This isn't about being girly, but rather about embracing a look that makes you feel good about yourself. Sometimes just shaving your legs or wearing your favorite sports jersey is enough to do this. So what are you waiting for? Rock those smooth legs, and Go Team, Go!

Create something: One day I decided to take a painting class. I'm no artist, so I had no idea what to expect, but I won a free class and wasn't about to waste it. I decided to paint a picture of my dog, Walker, and couldn't believe how much I enjoyed myself. For two hours I barely said a word as I concentrated on my brush strokes and shading.

For me, creating usually takes the form of writing, so it felt good to try something different. When I got home, I couldn't wait to show off my masterpiece and asked my husband to hang it up immediately. Now every time I look at it, I think about the day I went outside of my comfort zone and am reminded that not only am I capable of trying new things, but I can succeed at them as well.

These ten ideas don't even begin to scratch the surface of what's possible when you decide to care for yourself, but hopefully it's a start to get you thinking... and doing!

The self-care world is your oyster, my friend. Have a blast exploring it.

***

Before we move on to the next few chapters, the chapters about relationships, I need you to understand something very important:

Whether you're in a relationship right now or not, your love story has already begun.

Don't you see? Life is fluid. Everything is connected. The way you live now will impact the way you live in the future. What is going on in your life today is as much a part of your love story as what will happen after you meet your Someone Special. Nothing is separate here. All the chapters of your life are still a part of the same book.

And if I can't convince you to believe that your love story is already in motion, can I at least persuade you to love yourself now so that you can love someone else later? When you do happen to meet your Someone Special, they're going to want to hear all about what you've been up to. If all you have to say is, "Waiting for you," that'd be such a shame.

There's nothing wrong with you that must be fixed before you can start living your love story. Your love story starts now. In fact, it's already begun.

So do all you can to make it a good one.

Questions to consider:

Which of the ten self-care suggestions are you looking forward to trying?

In what ways do you struggle to see how your love story has already begun?

PART 2: LOVING SOMEONE ELSE

EXPECTING RESPECT

"If you expect respect from others, show it first to yourself. You can't expect from others what you don't give to yourself." –Shams Tabrizi

If self-worth is the foundation and self-ish practices are the frame, maybe expecting respect is the mailbox. Letters, cards, bills, and advertisements come in the mail every single day. It's up to you to decide which ones should be opened, which ones require a response, and which ones get tossed in the trash. Sometimes you don't have to even open a letter to know that it's junk mail. I mean, when was the last time you opened something from the Publisher's Clearinghouse?

Dating is kind of similar. After gaining a bit of experience and learning more about yourself, it becomes easier to decipher who seems to be a serious contender and who is not. Kissing a bunch of frogs is hardly fun, but it teaches us what to look for in a partner. We learn best from our mistakes.

I always say that expecting respect is the first rule of dating. Women who have a desire to be respected when they're dating want a kind partner more than they want a hot partner. They know that being single is a helluva lot better than being disrespected. A little bit of attention doesn't sway them from their standards. That's because they understand that attention and respect are not the same thing.

Please don't confuse someone's pursuit of you as respect because you're excited and tired of being alone. Regardless of whether or not you end up being with that person for the long haul, you deserve to be respected as soon as the first date begins. Give yourself permission to carry yourself in a way that communicates that.

I'm sure you've heard that we teach others how to treat us. It seems people really do follow our lead when it comes to these things. I mean, how likely is it that someone will treat you like crap if you never give them the opportunity to do so?

Now, don't get me wrong. I've already mentioned that the way other people treat you is not your responsibility. You cannot control or predict how others treat you, and you should never feel obligated to try. Rather than trying to manipulate someone else's behaviors, your time will be best spent doing two things: 1. showing other people what type of treatment is acceptable, starting with what type of treatment you accept from yourself and, 2. cutting your losses if their actions do not match up with your expectations.

The perfect time to think long and hard about how you want to be treated in a relationship is before you're even in one. Then you must commit to kicking anyone to the curb who seems disinterested in treating you properly. It's not just enough to want a respectful partner; you have to actually be willing to let go of relationships that do not support your well-being. This can be really hard to do when you're eager to meet someone new. Trust me. I've been there. Even so, it's a lot easier to cut your losses early on than to break up with someone you have deep feelings for.

There's a lot of junk mail out there in the world. But what you're waiting for is the total package.

And if the package exceeds your wildest dreams, it just might be worth the wait.

Question to consider:

What words or images come to mind when you think of respect? (It's okay if you think of Aretha Franklin!)

WHAT DOES RESPECT LOOK LIKE ANYWAY?

"The most attractive quality a man can have is respect. Respect for women, and respect for himself." -Nev Schulman

We all have different tastes when it comes to relationships, but there are a handful of characteristics that all healthy relationships have in common. Here's what respect in a relationship typically looks like:

Not abusive: It's completely normal to argue in a relationship, but there are clear boundaries you and your partner should never cross. Name-calling, physical violence, manipulation, and control are just a few examples.

Safe: Because human beings are imperfect and make mistakes, all relationships make us susceptible to pain every now and then. Even so, you should still feel generally safe in your relationship. For instance, you should feel confident that your partner isn't going to cheat on you or try to cause you physical or emotional pain.

Supportive: A supportive partner won't manipulate you into doing what he/she wants, but will encourage you to reach your dreams and pursue your own idea of happiness. It feels absolutely dreadful to be with someone who doesn't believe in you, knocks you down constantly, or tries to control you—these three things are the exact opposite of respect. With all of the negativity in the world, you're looking for a cheerleader, not a Debbie Downer.

Accepting: Being with someone who genuinely enjoys who you are and accepts you 100% pretty much rocks. Feeling free to be yourself without judgment is one of the best things about a healthy relationship. The greatest gift you can give the world is a really awesome version of yourself. Anyone you choose to date should really believe this.

***

So, here's the thing. Sometimes it takes a bit of time to determine whether a new relationship is healthy or not. People don't usually go on first dates with stickers on their foreheads that say "abusive", "not supportive", or "cheater". As Chris Rock says, "When you meet someone for the first time, you're not meeting them, you're meeting their representative."

Don't let this discourage you. Chances are, you're on your best behavior during the first couple of dates with a new person, too. One thing you can do is look out for red flags. These, along with your personal dating standards (more on this later), will help guide you as you get to know new people.

Here are a few red flags to be mindful of as you begin dating, courtesy of The Red Flag Campaign, an anti-abuse campaign I absolutely LOVE. (You can check them out at www.theredflagcampaign.org.)

Be on the lookout for potential partners who:

- Abuse alcohol or other drugs.

- Have a history of trouble with the law, get into fights, or break and destroy property.

- Don't work or go to school.

- Blame you for how they treat you, or for anything bad that happens.

- Abuse siblings, other family members, children, or pets.

- Put down people, including your family and friends, and/or call them names.

- Are always angry at someone or something.

- Try to isolate you and control whom you see and/or where you go.

- Nag you or force you to be sexual when you don't want to be.

- Cheat on you or have lots of partners.

- Are physically rough with you (push, shove, pull, yank, squeeze, restrain).

- Take your money or take advantage of you in other ways.

- Accuse you of flirting or "coming on" to others, and/or accuse you of cheating on them.

- Don't listen to you or show interest in your opinions or feelings.

- Ignore you, give you the silent treatment, or hang up on you.

- Lie to you, don't show up for dates, and maybe even disappear for days.

- Make vulgar comments about others in your presence.

- Blame all arguments and problems on you.

- Tell you how to dress or act.

- Threaten to kill themselves if you break up with them, or tell you that they cannot live without you.

- Experience extreme mood swings...tell you you're the greatest one minute and rip you apart the next minute.

- Tell you to shut up or tell you you're dumb, stupid, fat, or call you some other name (directly or indirectly).

- Compare you to former partners.

A few other things to look for? If your new beau buys you expensive gifts that make you feel uncomfortable, pressures you to agree to a monogamous relationship soon after meeting, says derogatory things about ex-partners or other women, expresses unreasonable jealousy when you interact with other people, and/ or places you on a pedestal, RUN. (Of course, if you feel like your safety might be in jeopardy, contact your local domestic violence center for support before doing so.)

Please note, many of these red flags will likely pop up after dating someone for a longer period of time. Toxic partners are often very charming in the beginning of relationships, looking to woo the people they are dating, in hopes of becoming closely attached early on in the relationship.

Additionally, it is incredibly important to allow other people to speak truth into your life. Your jealous single girlfriend might not ever speak highly of your partner, but if a large majority of your loved ones share the same negative opinion of the person you are seeing, I urge you to consider why. If you find yourself keeping details about your relationship a secret from your loved ones because you fear they will tell you to leave, be mindful of that as well. Sometimes it's hard to hear these suggestions from people close to us and it's hard to admit that your relationship might not be going as well as you'd hope. But at the end of the day, your close friends and family members truly do have your best interest in mind. And it is because they care about you and understand the depth of your worth that they want the very best for you.

In short, these red flags are bad news bears. Trust me when I say, you don't need any of that drama—life is hard enough as it is.

And unless you're a real housewife of New York, you definitely don't have to settle for that drama either.

Questions to consider:

Have you ever experienced any of the above red flags while in a relationship?

Have you ever committed any of the above red flags while in a relationship?

SHOULD YOU STAY OR SHOULD YOU GO?

"May your choices reflect your hopes, not your fears." –Nelson Mandela

If I got a dime for every time someone asked me this question, I'd be one rich woman.

I wish there was a simple way to answer this question, but you and I both know there isn't. Sometimes relationships are confusing. Certainly there are times when an outsider's opinion can help bring clarity to a convoluted situation. Generally, however, only the individuals actually involved in a relationship can make the ultimate decisions affecting its trajectory.

That is why rather than directly telling a woman what to do about her relationship, I ask her a series of questions to hopefully get her thinking about the situation more objectively. From there, she might feel a little more empowered to follow her intuition and make the best decision for her. If you are in a place where you are doubting your current relationship, here a few questions for you to honestly think about:

Does my partner exhibit any red flag behaviors? No one is perfect, but if your partner consistently engages in red flag behavior, it might be time to really think about the quality of your relationship. Are you truly happy? Do you feel safe? If toxic and abusive behavior is present within your relationship, there's a big chance that any growth you and your partner can achieve together will be inhibited.

(As I've previously mentioned, if you feel like your safety is being compromised, please seek the support of a local domestic violence agency. I know it can be hard to ask for help, but I urge you to try. Sometimes red flags can be difficult to deal with all on our own.)

What is my partner DOING to show me that they are working on their issues, are willing to work with me on our issues, and are committed to changing their unhealthy behaviors? Unlike some people, I do believe that people can change. While I would argue that the essence of each person often remains the same, I do feel that when individuals are committed to growth, they can do great things. In fact, I believe our capacity for growth is one of the best things about being a human.

Despite this, it's not just enough for your partner to tell you that things will be different and that love will get you through the hard times. In this case, actions speak louder than words. If you are working hard to make your relationship work, it's only fair that your partner is as well. A healthy relationship is a combined effort between two people.

It's equally important to note whether your partner is seeking support for any of their struggles. It's crucial for both you and your partner to have a reliable support network as you grow as individuals, and as a couple. You cannot be your partner's only source of support, and vice versa. Without support from others, it'll only be that much harder to leave if you ever decide to.

Additionally, if your partner does not have other healthy relationships to turn to in times of need, consider why. Because that's pretty telling.

If my partner were to stay the same forever, would I be okay with that? Are you in love with who your partner is now, or who your partner could be in the future? Regardless of whatever you and your partner are doing to improve your relationship, there is always the chance that they will not follow through on their promises. Knowing this, it is up to you to decide whether you can live with who they are now, not who they could be later.

There's absolutely nothing wrong with seeing potential in your partner, but please remember that in a relationship, they deserve to be accepted for who they are, just like anyone else. If you find your relationship unacceptable for the long-term and do not see your partner working hard to change that, I urge you to consider whether your relationship is truly sustainable.

If you are on the fence about your relationship, I'm sorry. I personally know how hard it is to go back and forth about someone you love. Months before breaking up with my ex-boyfriend, I couldn't stop thinking about all the pros and cons of staying in our relationship. I felt scared to leave and often used my confusion as an excuse to stay in an unhealthy situation. Many times I resorted to asking him if we could "take a break," rather than breaking up with him fully. I thought ripping off the Band-Aid slowly would lessen the pain, when in fact, it only made it worse. Our relationship was my security blanket and I didn't want to let it go. I thought that if I could just hold out for a little longer, the answer would come to me, clear as day. Naïvely, I held out hope, but my hope was based in fear.

The clear-as-day sign that I was waiting for actually occurred in the form of violence: The night my ex-boyfriend threatened me in a manner that still causes me to shudder today. In hindsight, it doesn't surprise me that I needed something drastic to happen in order for me to take drastic measures; I can be pretty hard-headed. Today, I am grateful that I was not seriously injured that night, or even worse, killed. I certainly would not want for either of these things to happen to you either. Please take care of yourself.

I think many women struggle to follow their intuition because they are wavering in confidence. They don't feel certain in their ability to successfully leave a relationship, be on their own, and heal from all the pain. Of course these are legitimate concerns. The reason why I do the work I do is because of these things.

Please know, however, that confidence usually comes after you take the leap, not before. If you're waiting until you feel ready to make a decision, you'll likely be waiting a long time. That hesitation you feel before making a life-changing decision is completely normal; it's reminding you that you're human. Instead of waiting until you feel confident, focus on building confidence. How do you do that? By understanding that you'll need a sufficient amount of time and practice after diving into something new before you fully adjust.

Sometimes we cling to comfortable situations and our hope that they will magically change is actually based in fear. Relationships should be full of hope and promise, but please honestly contemplate whether reality supports your hope. If what you see happening within the relationship seems to warrant the hope you feel, then by all means, continue trucking ahead. There are no guarantees when it comes to relationships, but I still believe they're worth it, as long as you do not daily feel like you're forcing a circle into a square.

If you do feel like you're forcing a circle into a square, ask yourself this: What is keeping me here?

I urge you to not hold on to the relationship for longer than you need to out of fear. Remember, your time is precious and life is short. When asking if you should stay or go, be very honest with yourself about what you need and what you deserve, not just what you want. Who you spend the rest of your life with and who you make babies with are two of the biggest decisions you will ever make in your life. Choose wisely.

Questions to consider:

If you are considering ending a relationship, what scares you most about doing so?

For each fear you can think of, name one hopeful opportunity that could arise as a result of ending your relationship.

BREAKUPS CAN BE WAKE-UPS

"All the broken hearts in the world still beat."
-Ingrid Michaelson

If you do end up deciding to leave a relationship, please know that I am proud of you. Leaving someone you love is an incredibly difficult decision and it's even harder to actually follow through with that decision. This new season of your life that you are about to embark upon will be filled with many trials, but many joys are ahead of you as well. And you have all the strength you need to get through it.

In her book *Eat, Pray, Love*, author Elizabeth Gilbert says, "Ruin is a gift. Ruin is the road to transformation." This quote expresses the main reason why I decided to become a breakup coach. I know firsthand how catastrophic the loss of love can be. Whether the end of a relationship was your choice or not, it can feel like your whole life has been ruined. Take me, for instance. Though several events of my first serious relationship were incredibly traumatic, I learned a ton from them. I also discovered my passion for helping heartbroken women and survivors of abuse as a result of my own abuse. All of that pain eventually turned into something good.

Some may scoff at the term "breakup coach", but I truly believe in the positive impact breakups can have on women, if we let them. "It's not just a breakup… it's a wake-up" isn't my tagline for nothing! I'm a firm believer in the fact that life-altering events can change us into better people. That's why I help women find silver linings, and where there seemingly are none, I help women to create them.

While my clients are adjusting to their new relationship status, I also help them make moves forward, in small ways at first. After breaking up with their ex-partner or being dumped by their ex-partner (and discussing the logistics of the breakup), the FIRST thing I recommend for my clients to do is consider following the No-Contact Rule: not speaking to or interacting with an ex-partner for at least two months, post-breakup.

I am a strong proponent of the No-Contact Rule for many reasons. First, it is incredibly hard to move on from the pain of a breakup if you're still interacting with your ex. Unless your split is unusually amicable, it will take some time to get used to your ex playing a different role in your life. Moving towards the future requires you to loosen your grip on the past. Cutting contact, even if only for a little bit, allows for a time of adjustment to a new reality.

It's equally important that you teach yourself how to respond with your head, rather than reacting with your heart. For instance, at any given moment, you may think it will feel good to talk to your ex. But if you end up crying your eyes out and begging them to take you back, you'll likely feel really embarrassed if they refuse. Cutting off contact for a bit will help you regain not only your strength, but also your clarity. After two months on your own, you may begin to see your relationship in a different light than before. As they say, hindsight is 20/20.

In his book *It's Called a Breakup Because It's Broken*, Greg Behrendt calls the No-Contact Rule the #1 commandment. According to Behrendt:

"This is our #1 commandment and it is hands down the most important thing you can do for yourself. The idea is to get him out of your system—and he's much less likely to continue to wield his power and stay under your skin if you don't have any contact. Furthermore, laying down the sixty-day rule gives you the opportunity to take control of a situation that has you reeling out of control. It's your chance to call the shots. We don't care if he (or you) still wants to be friends, if he still has some of your stuff, or if you were fused together in a welding accident. You can revisit all of these issues two months from now when you have some clarity."

Of course, you may have some extenuating circumstances to address. For instance, if you and your ex have children or work together, cutting off all contact will not be an option. In these cases, it's even more important to identify the boundaries that will help you keep your heart feel safe, while also tending to your responsibilities. Often times, close friends or family members can help us stay sane as we resolve custody issues. Lean on them as you navigate the murky waters ahead.

One way to help you be more successful with the No-Contact Rule is to write out a plan where you identify what boundaries you will maintain regarding contact with your ex. In your plan, be sure to address these things:

- Face-to-Face

- Texting (especially those late night texts)

- Phone calls

- Returning items to one another

- Anything else? (i.e. conversations about children)

After addressing these various scenarios in your plan, think about what you will do when you're feeling a little weak. Who will you contact instead of your ex-partner? What will you do instead (i.e. self-care activities)? Where can you shift your attention until the urge to make contact passes?

While I do recommend maintaining no contact at all, it's important that you know that it is you who owns your plan. No one, myself included, can tell you what is best for you. If you finish two months of not speaking with your ex and feel like you still need more time, that's fine. Take whatever time you need to heal and continue creating your new, fabulous life. By the same token, if you decide to maintain contact with your ex-partner, please do so because it feels right for you. Don't force yourself to maintain a friendship because of any pressure you may feel from others. When it comes to your boundaries, you get to call the shots. Remember: Your life, your rules.

Lastly, it's important that you show yourself grace in the case of any mishaps. If you commit to the No-Contact Rule, but end up texting your ex during a weak moment, you can always get back up and start again. Desiring comfort from someone who feels familiar to you is completely normal. There's no need to hate yourself or give yourself grief over a mistake. We all make them, right?

Instead, think about how contacting your ex made you feel. Here are some common emotions people typically feel after reconnecting with an ex-partner:

Comfort: Did you experience the comfort you hoped for? If you were physically intimate, did you enjoy the experience, or feel taken advantage of?

Longing: Are you wanting to get back together?

Sadness/Pain: Do you feel worse after the interaction?

Confusion: Are you wondering if you two made the right decision?

Relief: Do you feel confirmation that the relationship should be over?

Failure: Do you feel like you've taken a step back in your healing?

After processing your feelings, think about what you truly need. Was it helpful to your healing to experience whatever emotions your reconnection spawned? If not, what can you do to ensure you stick to your plan of no contact, so that the likelihood of you experiencing those negative emotions decreases?

Next, after discerning your level of commitment to the No-Contact Rule, it's important to identify your cheerleaders. In these next few weeks of pain and confusion, who will be your support system? Whether your relationship was incredibly toxic or not, you might benefit from professional support from a therapist or breakup coach (ahem!). Additionally, if your relationship was toxic, I highly recommend hiring a professional who can help you process your trauma.

One of the best things I did after my breakup was join a support group for survivors of domestic violence. I attended this group on Wednesday evenings and soon started looking forward to attending every week. The shame and embarrassment I felt slowly melted away as I learned the stories of other women whose lives were also affected by abusive men. I guess I knew deep down that I wasn't alone, but actually hearing their stories and seeing their faces confirmed it. Leaving my ex gave me the space to accomplish some great things, but this new sisterhood is what gave me the motivation I needed to accomplish those great things.

One lady moved into her own place after many years of marriage and was loving it. Another graduated from school and moved into her first home with her children. Another gal was finally clean for several months and had no desire to get back with her ex, as she knew his presence in her life only interfered with her sobriety.

Like me, these women were facing their own challenges and using their pain as a catapult into greatness. Each week I left my group feeling inspired. For those four years I felt so alone. But I was not alone.

You aren't either.

Third, I urge my clients to shift their focus away from the "ruin" and towards the "transformation." More specifically, we work on goal-setting, as seasons of transition can be excellent times to challenge yourself in different ways. As a newly single woman, it may feel like you have a lot of time and energy to spare. If you do not find productive ways to channel this energy, you may end up throwing frequent pity parties, drinking way too much alcohol, or eating ice cream for dinner every night.

If you really want to bounce back after a hard breakup, a great place to start is with your internal aspirations. What have you always wanted to accomplish, but felt would be too out of reach? Perhaps there is a hobby you can explore or a milestone you can reach. When one of my closest friends found herself single after a long-term relationship, she decided to start salsa dancing. She was so interested in salsa that she even went to lessons by herself. Years later, she still has a deep love for salsa dancing—and a husband to dance with her on Friday nights.

Not a fan of dancing? Here are some other ideas for goals to focus on after a breakup:

Move your body. Start yoga, running, Zumba, or kickboxing. You can even enter a race or competition to really focus on your improvement.

Learn something new. Take an art class, like painting or ceramics. Order Rosetta Stone and "parlez-vous Francais." (Bonus points if you plan a trip to Paris afterward.)

Start a project. Begin a quilt or scrapbook. Help your parents clear out their attic. Start a blog.

Volunteer. Join Big Brothers/Big Sisters, or visit your local animal shelter.

***

Lastly, and probably most importantly, I encourage my clients to feel. One of the hardest and crummiest parts of heartbreak is the pain. Because we are humans, we are inclined to avoid pain at all costs. This is why we delay breakups or distract ourselves from pain with alcohol, sex, or food. Unfortunately, however, when it comes to healing, allowing ourselves to feel and embrace our pain is a necessary step.

Grief causes us to feel a whirlwind of emotions, which can be very overwhelming at first. Once you realize that though the pain feels like it's killing you, it actually is not, you can start to let yourself feel it, each time with less and less intensity. Sometimes letting go emotionally can be a very scary thing to do, but the only way past pain is through it. And don't think for one moment that showing your emotions is a sign of weakness. Feelings are like volcanic lava—if you don't let them flow, eventually you'll erupt.

For me, it took one little quote to completely shift my perspective on pain. While watching an episode of *Oprah*, a grieving guest said the words: "You have to go through the fire of grief." For some reason, this sentence really stuck with me. For so long I tried to be strong, trying to prove to my closest loved ones that even though my plans were derailed, I still had everything under control. I never realized that my avoidance of pain and grief was actually complicating my healing process. My need for control was suffocating me.

That night, I finally allowed myself to cry, and I mean, really cry. After I was done, I felt amazing. For many weeks later, I cried myself to sleep every night and woke up feeling a bit stronger every morning until one night, I could fall asleep without sobbing.

When healing from heartache, it is important that you let yourself cry. Don't fight your tears and don't fight any other emotions either. If you feel angry, let yourself feel that anger. If you feel jealous, acknowledge that too. Let those emotions wave over you as they are meant to and talk yourself through it in a compassionate way. Don't let a whole day pass by without caring for yourself in a way you need.

The truth is, healing happens over the course of time—not in a specific moment or way. Healing is a journey where sometimes you take three steps forward and a day later take four steps back. But it's not just a journey; it's your journey. We are all different, and so are our healing journeys. There are no specific steps to healing, so what helps someone else heal might not be very helpful to you. What matters most is that you are constantly checking in with your intuition, staying in touch with your needs, and being kind to yourself.

You may feel ruined now, but just you wait for the transformation. It will blow you away.

I promise.

***

P.S. To the ladies who've recently been dumped, cheated on, or lied to:

I'm sorry. The pain of betrayal is unlike any other. Your breakup was likely not something you planned for or even wanted, which I know only contributes to the hurt. It's hard to accept that such major life decisions can be made without our input—that one day, a simple sentence can change everything.

I know there's absolutely nothing I can say to take the pain away, so I won't try. When life feels unfair, the last thing we want to hear is a lecture on how "everything happens for a reason." So don't worry; I'm won't go there.

What feels most productive to me is that I encourage you to do three things. These things certainly won't fix the pain, but they should help.

First, find safety. Life might feel incredibly unsafe right now, especially if you've been betrayed by someone you thought loved you. Your whole understanding of how the world works may have been shaken, which means you'll need to develop a new understanding. Who are the folks in your life who will let you be a mess without judging you? Those are the people you need to be around. Figure out where you can simply be yourself without having to worry about keeping your guard up.

Second, make your well-being your top priority. Sure, other people still matter, but now is the time to really love and care for yourself. Please note: there is a difference between tending to your wounds until they heal and demanding retribution because you've been wronged. Don't fester in bitterness until you start exhibiting entitlement. Focus on the fact that you need to get well again. Do the healthy things you need to do until that happens.

Then, be mad. Be mad, be sad, be jealous—be whatever you need to be, as long as you remember that negative feelings don't justify negative behaviors. (For example, even though it would feel really awesome, you're not allowed to key your ex's car. If you end up on Judge Judy, your deep pain will not stop her from screaming at you. Revenge is a big no-no. This is one major detail that Carrie Underwood fails to mention.)

Yes, let yourself experience every awful emotion you can imagine. It's okay; you're allowed. But not for forever. At some point you'll need to shower, get to work, and eat something. You can't lay on the couch all day, asking yourself how your ex could be so cruel. You may never find the answers to the questions you're asking over and over again. Eventually, you'll have to be okay with that.

Dwelling in negative emotions causes us to live our lives with a chip on our shoulder, thinking that it will protect us. Healing is the process of chiseling away at that chip, knowing that it cannot protect us.

Instead, the challenge is to fully experience your sadness while fully understanding that you are much more than your sadness. If you find yourself really struggling with this some days, give yourself a time limit on how long you will let yourself actively mope, cry, and scream. When it's time to stop moping for the day, start getting ready for your next activity (hint, hint: a self-care activity, if you can swing it). You can feel as sad as you want to while you're getting yourself out of bed, but what's most important is that you get yourself out of bed. And as you're doing so, repeat this phrase to yourself out loud:

"I will get through this. My heart is brave."

One day, you'll believe it. Until then, lean on your safe support network. And know that regardless of any shame or embarrassment you may feel, you're not in this alone. You're never alone, my friend.

***

Dr. Elisabeth Kübler-Ross was an American psychiatrist and author best known for her five stages of grief theory. She wrote a ton about loss and mourning, but one of my favorite quotes by her comes from the book, *Death: The Final Stage of Growth*:

"The most beautiful people we have known are those who have known defeat, known suffering, known struggle, known loss, and have found their way out of the depths. These persons have an appreciation, a sensitivity, and an understanding of life that fills them with compassion, gentleness, and a deep loving concern. Beautiful people do not just happen."

During this time of deep hurt, please remember that your pain is not futile. Your beauty is not just "happening" out of mid-air; it's being made. As you make your way out of the depths, you are being made.

And that's why this is not just a breakup.

It's a wake-up.

Questions to consider:

Have you ever followed the No-Contact Rule after breaking up with an ex? Did it help you? How was it scary?

Do you struggle to let yourself feel painful emotions? How can you help yourself become more accepting of pain in your own life?

If you are currently going through a breakup, what is ONE goal you are going to start focusing on? What next steps do you need to take in order to make sure you reach that goal?

If you're experiencing heartbreak right now, you may be asking yourself why it happened. Instead of focusing on why, have you thought about what you are learning? If not, what are you learning?

SOME THOUGHTS ON DATING

"It's all about falling in love with yourself and sharing that love with someone who appreciates you, rather than looking for love to compensate for a self-love deficit." –Eartha Kitt

When I was nineteen years old, I decided to make a list of all the qualities I wanted my future husband to have.

Basically, I wanted a Christian man who loved hiking, listening to music, and watching movies. He had to be a good listener, active in his church, and a couple years older than me. My husband would also have a good sense of humor, brown hair, and a few muscles (because of all the hiking, of course). If he knew how to drive stick, that'd be great since I wanted to learn how to drive stick, too. And before asking me to marry him, my future husband would talk to my father first, have my best friend to help him pick the ring, and propose to me as I swung on a porch swing and sipped on some lemonade. Then, after two or three years of wedded bliss, we'd have four children, I'd be a stay-at-home mama, and we'd all live happily ever after.

It's a little embarrassing to admit all of this to you, but I won't be offended if you think I was a bit of a psycho. It sounds pretty ridiculous even when I think about it. Who did I think I was, creating my own made-to-order husband?

The thing is, I know a lot of gals who have similar lists floating in their heads, whether they'll admit it or not. It's as if they know everything about their husband before they've even met them. And while I admire thorough planning, I'm not certain these lists are very helpful. In fact, in many ways, I find them harmful.

How about, instead of focusing on physical char-acteristics and other minor details, you start thinking long and hard about how you want to feel in your romantic relationships? Do you know how your future spouse will treat you and others? Does it matter how they act during conflict and crisis, if they work hard on their own personal issues, or if they treat life like the gift that it is?

I hope so. Sure, physical attraction and shared interests are important, but if that rich hottie you're seeing is also a huge jerk, what's the point? That is why answering many of the above questions will help you set your standards, focusing mainly on how you want to be treated by your future partner.

Standards are important. Standards help us in our quest to be respected. Certainly it's okay to want to marry a non-smoker who goes to church and likes music, but if you have no idea how you want this person to treat you, you are probably getting lost in the details.

Your job is not to dream up your future spouse before you've even met them. Besides, don't you want to marry someone who exceeds your wildest dreams? No, your job is to get clear on how this person carries themselves. Then your next job is to hold onto your standards as you date new people.

So many heartbroken women regret staying in bad relationships for far too long. Without confidently knowing how they want to be treated, confusion overwhelms them when their relationship turns sour. Deciding to leave someone you love can be a tough decision, even when the relationship is toxic, exhausting, or stagnant. Giving yourself permission to leave a situation that is not serving you before you get in too deep is vital.

Having clear standards doesn't mean you'll never experience heartache and holding tight to your standards won't make you immune to pain. You will, however, know what it's like to stay true to yourself.

And it's staying true to ourselves that helps us cope with pain.

I'm not one to tell women to set high standards either. Personally, I'm not even sure what exactly that means. As an adult, this is all about your life and your rules. I am in no place to judge whether your standards are too high or not high enough than the next person. Therefore, rather than encouraging you to set your standards high, I'm much more interested in you setting standards that resonate with your essence. (Hint: this is where your self-ish practice of self-awareness will really come in handy!)

What works for you may not work for someone else and vice versa. As they say (or maybe I just made this up): one woman's boring first date is another woman's lifelong companion. What matters most is that you can identify the difference between being open to dating different people and being unwilling to settle for treatment that does not match up with your standards.

So when it comes to setting standards, don't let anyone tell you yours are too high or not high enough. Instead, focus on how you want to be treated. Then, keep believing that you deserve that treatment, even when all your friends are getting married or you've been dumped for the umpteenth time. That's the key to being respected: holding out hope for the best and healthiest version of what it is you really want, and fully believing that you deserve nothing less.

**

This might surprise you, but even after experiencing abuse, I still continued to date unkind men.

For me, dating was something I did haphazardly. After breaking up with my ex-boyfriend, I was frantic to find someone new, and this goal was more important to me than taking sufficient time to learn from my past mistakes. As a result, I gave any man who showed interest in me a chance. This meant that on many occasions, I dated men who weren't very nice to me for much longer than I probably should have.

I dated some real duds. And yet, even after realizing they were duds, I struggled with letting them go. Like many of us, feeling lonely was really hard for me. But back then I made the mistake of thinking that finding someone new would magically cure my loneliness, rather than learning healthy ways to cope with it. As a result, my love life struggled severely.

Unfortunately, the dozens of dating manuals I was reading led me to believe otherwise. Rather than focusing on the inside, I was too distracted by attaining validation from the outside. I was stuck and needed help. I needed to learn how to love myself, expect respect, and date in a healthy way.

There is absolutely no shame in kissing a few frogs from time to time. Dating is all about trial and error, so it's assumed not every date will be a smashing success. But when you meet a frog who doesn't treat you very nicely, it's best to throw the little guy back into the pond.

That's where frogs belong.

I remember the days when I'd be smitten by anyone with an XY chromosome and nice eyes. If he showed interest in me, I was game. This really interfered with my ability to view the men I was dating as individuals. Instead, he was someone to impress—a potential end to my miserable singleness.

That said, it's no wonder that dating used to cause me such stress. Because I was so insecure and had little self-worth, I constantly felt like I was under scrutiny. Instead of enjoying the men I was seeing, I obsessively analyzed every text, every outfit, and every single word. If I didn't hear from someone within a "reasonable" amount of time, I'd assume he was losing interest in me and that I was doomed to be alone forever. I needed to learn how to enjoy dating (which only happened after I learned to love myself).

As I previously mentioned, I made the mistake of trying to convince my first boyfriend to like me. Years later, I had not yet broken this habit. I worked hard to convince men to like me, in order to prove I was worthy of their attention. I did all I could to appear desirable, whether it aligned with my essence or not. That's why I read so many dating books, spent loads of money on "sexy" clothes and shoes, and counted each calorie that entered my mouth. It never occurred to me that earning someone else's love was the exact opposite of what I really wanted. No, what I really wanted was to be loved and accepted for who I already was.

At the end of the day, that's all any of us wants, really: To know that we can be loved and accepted for who we really are. These thoughts by author and researcher Dr. Brené Brown about belonging describe the struggle many of us experience in our search for those two things:

"For example, contrary to what most of us think: Belonging is not fitting in. In fact, fitting in is the greatest barrier to belonging. Fitting in, I've discovered during the past decade of research, is assessing situations and groups of people, then twisting yourself into a human pretzel in order to get them to let you hang out with them. Belonging is something else entirely—it's showing up and letting yourself be seen and known as you really are—love of gourd painting, intense fear of public speaking, and all. Many of us suffer from this split between who we are and who we present to the world in order to be accepted. (Take it from me: I'm an expert fitter-inner!) But we're not letting ourselves be known, and this kind of incongruent living is soul-sucking."

Many of us settle for fitting in, though what we truly crave is belonging. I think this happens a lot when we date and it causes us to settle in other ways too. I mean, how many of us have ever invested in friends who didn't treat us nicely or stayed in jobs that do not align with our values? (Slowly raises own hand.) Unfortunately, circumstances like these are often not built upon authenticity and ultimately, do us a disservice when we compromise ourselves for their sake.

Healthy dating, on the other hand, has very little to do with convincing someone else to like us and changing ourselves in order to feel special. Instead of pining for attention, healthy dating actually occurs when we are focused on these four things:

1. Being authentic: Changing who you are to get someone to like you is not only exhausting, but it feels bad to not be accepted for who you truly are. Know thyself and then be thyself, my friend.

2. Having fun: Don't let the anxiety of dating overshadow the opportunity to have fun with someone new. Let yourself really enjoy the movie, savor the dinner, or celebrate all of your bowling strikes.

3. Connecting with someone new: Practice your investigation skills! Obviously you don't want to go overboard and appear nosey, but asking thoughtful questions will not only allow you to learn more about your date, but also connect with them. Share fun facts about yourself too. You can totally express how awesome you are without spilling your guts.

4. Staying in the present: This means not planning your wedding or naming your unborn babies after two or three dates! Think about how you feel in the moment. Does being with this person make you feel good inside? Why or why not?

Ultimately, healthy dating is all about dating from a place of wholeness, not desperation. When you view yourself as an incomplete person in need of a relationship to complete you, you are setting yourself up for failure. No one should feel responsible for completing you; that's an exorbitant amount of pressure to put on someone else, especially a stranger you just started dating.

Your other option is to date, focusing on connection, fun, and growth. Rather than wondering if your date likes you, think about whether or not you like your date. Can you list specific things that set your date apart from other people? What makes your crush unique? In what ways do you connect, non-sexually? What is it exactly about them that gives you butter-flies?

If you can be clear on those answers, then perhaps you've found your match. Maybe you'll hit it off and be together forever. Or, maybe you'll hit it off and be together for a few weeks. Just remember, no matter what the future holds, you can totally handle it. Because your worth and well-being does not depend solely on the success of any one relationship.

Questions to consider:

How do you want to be treated in a relationship? How does this match up with what you've experienced in your love life thus far?

Is it important to you that your partner loves children? Do you want someone who is close to your family? Should they work hard in their career? What else is important to you in a relationship?

How will you stay true to your values as you date new people?

What is your favorite part of dating? What is your least favorite part of dating?

How can you focus on your favorite parts of dating and calm down a bit about your least favorite parts?

REJECTION: A GIFT THAT DOESN'T FEEL TOO GOOD

"I don't want anyone who doesn't want me."

–Oprah Winfrey

The other day I was thinking about my past dating adventures. Man, there have been a bunch. After breaking up with my ex, I worked hard to fill the void he left in my life. For a while this meant going out every weekend, in search of someone who could distract me from the loneliness and discomfort I felt from being alone. I haven't had many serious relationships, but I dated a lot before meeting my husband.

As I'm sure you could guess, I didn't have much luck with filling this void, largely because it was a void only I could fill. I was so scared of myself...of facing my own issues and dealing with them. I guess I thought meeting the perfect man would somehow save me from having to do either of those things. I had such high hopes for these complete strangers—hope they really didn't deserve.

I recently decided to do a little Facebook-stalking to see what a few of these guys are up to these days,

Respected

curious how our lives drifted apart. Before I would get so bummed when relationships didn't work out, but now I see that none of those men were very good for me anyway. I wanted some proof, so I conducted a little experiment. Here's what I learned:

Bachelor #1 was someone I dated for a few weeks. He pursued me relentlessly and eventually I gave in—I even had Thanksgiving dinner with him and his roommates. Imagine my surprise when I logged into Facebook and saw that he was in a relationship with someone else, just one day after we hung out at my house and he asked me to be his girlfriend! I didn't feel quite ready for that, but the fact that he was seeing someone else while he was seeing me was completely shocking. I was heartbroken and texted him incessantly to convince him to break up with her. (That was not my proudest moment.)

Nowadays it looks like he's living the dream in Los Angeles, trying to build a career as a cartoonist. I wish him luck, even though he was a major jerk to me.

Bachelor #2 and I went on two dates after meeting in a bar. I was drunk when we met, but sober enough to see how hot he was. (What can I say? Tattoos and piercings make me weak in the knees.) After our first date, I was already naming our unborn children, but I guess he wasn't on the same page because after making plans to hang out with me for a third time, he never showed up. It's all good though, since he looks really happy with his fiancé now. They have a cat and he posts about baseball a lot. I'm more of a dog person and think baseball is kind of boring, so I guess it all worked out.

Bachelor #3 and I had the most fun first date ever. After getting dinner and drinks, we played *Rock Band* in his apartment for a few hours—he played guitar and I sang. I was so smitten by him and was pretty sad when he never asked me out again. Anyway, he lives with his girlfriend now...in Australia! Clearly he wasn't kidding when he mentioned his adventurous spirit, a trait him and I do not share.

Bachelor #4 is someone I continued to speak with after we stopped dating each other. It only took a matter of time until I learned of our major differences. Enter Exhibit A:

Him: Hey!

Me: Hey! Anything new?

Him: I'm the same. Working and training a lot. Having sex.

Me: That's good that you're working and training. Be safe when you're having sex.

Him: I'm mostly just sleeping with one person.

Me: Mostly? Lol.

Him: Yeah, I mean, I've got my hoes, but I've been sleeping with just this one for the last few months.

Me: *shocked and silent*

I typically spend my time with people who respect women a little more than this, so in hindsight I understand why it never worked out with him. Still, while we were dating, I was so determined to get him to like me. (I wish back then I knew that convincing a guy to like me isn't as fun as him actually liking me.)

So what's the point of all of this? I guess my point is this: Rejection can be a precious gift. While dating each of these men, getting them to like me was all that mattered. The thought of their rejection absolutely frightened me, so I did all I could to avoid it.

After failing yet another time to get a man to love me and subsequently "save" me, I decided to take a break from it all. I spent my time focusing on work and my studies and growing more comfortable with being single. About six months later, when I felt more ready to get back into the dating game, I decided to join OK-Cupid. Two weeks after that, I met my husband. While

I don't believe I cracked the code to dating, I do know I was in a much better place to meet Dan when I did—I was more confident, less desperate, and all around happier. I liked that Dan liked me, the real me, but my entire well-being didn't depend on it.

***

What if we viewed the people in our "Dating Hall of Lame" not as jerks who rejected us, but as bearers of important lessons? And what if we learned to trust rejection, instead of resisting it like the plague? Rejection can be a guide, one of many, if we learn to embrace it. Sure it stings at first, but many times, rejection has our best interest in mind.

As I've mentioned, I think dating could much more fun if we focused on getting to know our dates, instead of desperately pining for their love and approval. In my experience, desperation was often a surefire way to receive the opposite. The pressure we put on ourselves to find a savior is suffocating. The pressure we put on strangers to save us is unfair.

Yes, I'm glad I didn't end up dating any of the above bachelors for any extended period of time. In hindsight I can see that in spite of my poor judgment, I dodged some bullets; I'm not living in Australia, cleaning a litter box, or being dragged to baseball games. For all of those things, I am grateful.

The point of this experiment was never to judge those men for their life choices though. Originally, I wanted to better understand why those relationships never flourished. But now I see that the reason why has very little to do with them and much more to do with me. My life unfolded as it should, and continues to unfold.

And in many ways, I think it's unfolding rather nicely.

I wish the very same for you.

Questions to consider:

Who's in your Dating Hall of Lame? What lessons have they taught you?

GIRLFRIEND OF THE YEAR

"Pray that when you meet someone who has a deep and true capacity to love you, you've developed to the point where you can accept it." –Tracy McMillan

In the beginning of this book I mentioned that one of the biggest things that sets my work apart from other relationship coaches is that I'm not solely focused on helping women find healthy relationships. I help women actively participate in healthy relationships.

A big part of this is helping women cultivate healthy relationships with themselves—relationships that can serve as a model for other relationships in their lives. The other big part of this is helping women understand what healthy relationships actually look like.

It's not enough to set your standards and pray hard that one day you'll meet someone wonderful who will support you and love you. Yes, you deserve support and love, but so does your future partner. The question is: Are you in a place where you can truly give that to someone else?

Most of the women I know, either professionally or personally, have been hurt by men in the past. As a result, they really struggle with trusting other people, especially in romantic relationships. They wonder if they will be cheated on again or if the loving confessions are sincere. Opening up their hearts again pretty much terrifies them.

I get it. As a recovering control freak and partner abuse survivor, trust is not my forte. Each day I have to intentionally practice letting my guard down and letting my husband in. Some days are harder than others, depending on how scared and anxious I'm feeling. (It's odd, but even when I so strongly desire to experience his love, in hopes that it will "fix" me, I still sometimes have an urge to resist it.)

I've often wondered if my past trauma and current control issues mean my husband is responsible for reassuring me whenever I may "need" it. Do I get to read through text messages on his phone whenever I feel like it? Do I really need to call him ten times a day to make sure he's not leading a double life, like my ex-boyfriend was? Is it okay for me to seek constant affirmation from him because men in my past made me feel worthless?

Nope.

Any betrayal, trauma, or heartache you've faced will likely affect any future relationships you choose to enter. A loving partner will certainly care about the hurt you've experienced in the past and do their best to take that hurt into account when interacting with you. However, it is not the job of your current partner to pay for the mistakes of your past partner. Your desire to never be hurt again cannot override your partner's autonomy within your relationship.

In other words, you don't get to be crazy, needy, desperate, or controlling just because someone hurt you in the past.

Honestly, it's your job to work on your issues before and after you meet someone new. (That's why the first section of this book is titled "Loving You"). It isn't fair to ask your new partner to work on your issues for you so that you don't have to face them. If you want to be in a loving, healthy relationship someday, you'll need to be a loving, healthy individual. When it comes to relationships, you can't expect from someone else what you're unable to give them. You won't be able to recognize it.

Equip yourself to be Girlfriend of the Year. Deal with your fears now so that you can gradually let your guard down to someone who seems worthy. Familiarize yourself with the relationship red flags so that you don't get into the habit of committing any of those errors yourself. Perhaps you're not a fighter, so you'd never hit your partner. But if you're constantly accusing your partner of cheating on you, that's pretty abusive too. And it's that type of behavior that will hinder you from contributing in the positive health of your relationship.

If you're trying to win the Girlfriend of the Year Award, here are a few other things to avoid:

Telling your partner how to act, what decisions to make, or how to spend their time: If they ask for your opinion on these things, then certainly help them out. But it's not your job to mold your partner into who you think they should be. Your job is to accept them as they are and encourage them as they grow.

Reading your partner's messages or emails: If your partner is going to be unfaithful to you, they are going to do so regardless of how often you check their phone and email. Screening their messages is actually only giving you a false sense of control and fostering a very unhealthy culture within your relationship. Instead of reading their messages behind their back, address the underlying issues that cause you to want to read them in the first place.

Not speaking up: Trying to avoid conflict by not saying what is on your mind is inauthentic. Let yourself shine by expressing yourself. Doing so is imperative if you want to deepen a true connection with someone. The people who really care about you will want to hear what's on your mind.

Forgetting about the other important people in your life: Please, for the love of all things holy, keep your friends in the loop. Don't disappear on them just because you're making out with someone new and exciting. It's tempting to choose cuddling over spin class or to ditch girl's night for a hot date, but don't make a habit of it. You will need your loved ones in the future, probably sooner than you'd like to admit. Besides, anyone worth dating is going to encourage you to stay close with your buddies because they know they cannot effectively be your everything.

Losing who you are: Good girlfriends know that in order to cultivate a thriving relationship, they must care for themselves, tend to their needs, and create a life outside of their relationship. Don't lose your identity or sacrifice who you are for the sake of your partner.

Trying to save your partner: We've all got issues. Some of us are more willing to acknowledge and work on our issues than others. Good girlfriends are awesome at supporting their partners as they work on their issues and try to improve their lives, but they don't put in more work than their partner does. That's because they know that people only change when they want to and feel ready. And they know that it isn't their job to "fix" their partner.

Pushing your own agenda: If you're set on getting married by the time you're 25 so you can have your first kid at 27 and try for your second by 29 and get back into the workforce around 33, perhaps you should relax. The trajectory of your relationship should not depend solely on your biological clock or your desire to plan a wedding. When making major life decisions, like, you know, marriage and babies, it's important that you and your partner communicate honestly with one another to develop a plan that works for the both of you. Your partner isn't along for the ride or obligated to propose just so you can get a move on your life goals. Either trust that your partner will propose when the time is right or have a well-needed heart-to-heart if things are taking too long, but stop the nagging. Pressure is the ultimate romance-killer.

If you do want to win the Girlfriend of the Year award someday, try to do these things instead (all ideas courtesy of a few of my Facebook friends):

"My girlfriend dresses me (not literally). Without her, my wardrobe would be nothing but sneakers, blue jeans, and superhero t-shirts. Thanks to her I can successfully pass myself off as a grown-up in public."

"My wife holds my hand, leaves me cute notes in the morning, and makes sure I have a snack if it's going to be a long day at work."

"My girlfriend is patient with me, communicates well during good and bad times, shows in many ways she cares (by asking how my day was to getting me my favorite candy bar), tries her best to understand my perspective but also challenges me to understand others, wants to know/care about the important people in my life, makes me feel enough, and encourages me in my faith."

"Oh...I don't think I'm allowed to say what awesome things she does on Facebook. ;-)"

"My wife always tells a joke if we're on the brink of arguing. Always makes us laugh! And she supports my writing."

"My girlfriend makes me laugh and proves everyday how much she cares. She listens to every word I say no matter how stupid it is. She scratches my back for me, even though she doesn't like to, but she knows I love it. She lets me have my hobbies which are overbearing at times and doesn't complain about it. She makes the stupid little duck face because I think it's hot for some reason. While I was in school, she left notes on my truck on the days I had tests. When it's the right one, everything they do is perfect."

Respected

"I love how passionate my wife is (even if it's annoying to me) and how strong she is through all she has dealt with. She puts others first no matter what and that always amazes me."

"I had a girlfriend who packed me a lunch for work several days a week. It seems so small and simple and stupid, but she put in food that was healthier than I would eat normally and sometimes she even put in a note to either tell me how much she loved me or to give me some background information on something she wanted to discuss later on and stuff like that."

"My wife asks people on social media what makes them awesome mates, then she adopts all of the best ones and applies them to our relationship and becomes a super-hero type lover." (That one is from my husband. This should give you a glimpse into what I'm dealing with.)

Questions to consider:

What is your favorite thing about being someone's girlfriend?

What are a few things you need to work on in your life in order to be a better girlfriend?

MYTH BUSTERS: MARRIAGE EDITION

"A journey is like marriage. The certain way to
be wrong is to think you control it."
–John Steinbeck

"My happiness grows in direct proportion to my
acceptance, and in inverse proportion to my
expectations." –Michael J. Fox

I'm going to assume that if you're reading this
book, you probably want to get married or re-married
someday (if you're not already married).

If this is the case, my question for you is this:
Why?

Do you yearn for companionship? Do you really
want to be a mother? Are you hoping to share your life
with someone? Do you like the idea of growing old
with someone else, just like Noah and Allie did in *The
Notebook*? Do you think marriage will make you happy? Are your parents pressuring you to find someone?
Are you hoping that finding a spouse will help you
financially?

There are a million and one reasons people want to get married. I'm not going to spend time judging any of those reasons, but it's worth mentioning that the reasons we get married cause us to form expectations about marriage. This is completely normal, which can also make the adjustment to marriage a little tricky. Why? Because most of the time, life doesn't line up with our expectations.

Whether it's in good or bad ways, life is always surprising us. We don't always get what we want and when that happens, we wind up disappointed. While I believe marriage is a worthwhile endeavor, I can also attest to the fact that it's filled with disappointment. My therapist likes to say that newly married people have a lot of grief work to do. As they adjust to a new life, they also have to grieve the lives they will never get to live with their new spouse.

For instance, my husband is a white man and I am a black female. Most days I love being in an interracial marriage, but some days it can be quite difficult. Our different backgrounds mean we must be extra careful in the ways we communicate, especially about race. There have been times when I've observed my parents, two black people, and wondered what it's like to be married to someone of the same race. Growing up in the sixties, I know my parents have experienced their fair share of racism together. But I also know that they can't relate to the stares Dan and I sometimes get when we're out in public. It may sound silly, but I've questioned whether it's easier to raise children or find a church to attend when you're married to someone of the same race.

If all goes as planned, I won't know what it's like to raise black children with a black man. I will continue to work hard at my marriage with my white husband and hopefully one day, we will raise biracial children together. And of course I am excited about our future together; if I wasn't, I wouldn't have married him in the first place! I absolutely adore my husband. But I'd be lying if I said that I've never imagined what life would be like if I had married a black man. I didn't realize it when I walked down the aisle, but slowly I've had to mourn that life I'll never live.

No matter how wonderful your marriage ends up being someday, the start of a new chapter in your life will mean the end of an old one. When you start to compare your expectations with reality, you may experience some frustration. In fact, I'd bet money on the fact that you will.

While expectations are completely normal to have, it's important not to cling too tightly to them. If you haven't already, take some time to explore the reasons why you want to get married and what you expect from marriage. High expectations will likely yield high disappointment. Remember, no relationship outside of the one with yourself is going to save you, not even marriage. Marriage cannot guarantee you happiness. Happiness is a choice you must make on your own.

So instead of clinging to your expectations of marriage, I strongly recommend you cling tightly to these things:

- Your self-worth

- Your self-ish practices, especially your self-care routine

- Your standards

- Your friends and family members who help you feel loved and safe

- Your desire for nothing less than respect

Go ahead, fantasize about your wedding day. Watch *Four Weddings* and let your mind wander a bit. But keep the daydreaming in check and stay focused on your own personal growth. Because (as I'm sure you know) marriage is so much more than a fairytale. It's a daily decision and partnership between two respected equals.

***

Sometimes it's hard for me to not be angry when I think about how our society approaches marriage. The wedding industry is a multi-billion dollar industry and if you turn on your television right now, I bet you could find at least one show about finding the perfect wedding dress, competing for a free honeymoon, or dealing with a bridezilla. It's crazy to me how one day somehow overshadows the lifetime of hard work ahead of newlyweds.

I suppose I'm showing my bias a bit. I'm not the biggest fan of weddings, evidenced by the fact that only sixteen people were invited to ours. Yes, I'll openly admit that I've seen many episodes of *Say Yes to the Dress* and even worked at a national wedding gown retailer for almost two years. Perhaps it is because of these experiences that I have little patience for it all.

Or maybe it's because of the struggles my friends and I have faced as newlyweds. Like most people, we had clear images in our minds of what marriage would be like. When those images didn't pan out, we had to re-adjust. (But only after complaining to each other for a bit first, of course.)

If you're nowhere close to getting married, feel free to skim through the next few pages. But when the time comes for you to walk down the aisle, promise me you'll come back to this chapter. I wish so very badly someone had gone over these myths with me before I tied the knot. Consider yourself lucky to learn these lessons well before you need to.

A few myths about marriage and commitment:

It will complete you: There are a million and one parts of your life that come together in such a unique way to make you who you are. This means your wholeness does not boil down to any one thing, especially whether or not you're in a relationship. A loving partner will certainly add to your life, but shouldn't be responsible for completing it. Regardless of your stance on soul mates, viewing yourself as deficient or lacking because of your relationship status is a very unhealthy way to live. Give yourself permission to believe you are whole right this second, whether you are married or single.

I once wrote a blog post on this subject that went viral on the *Huffington Post*. Because our wedding was a small and intimate occasion, my husband and I hosted a large reception for our one-year anniversary. About 150 of our closest friends and family members were in attendance and we both felt very blessed to celebrate the end of our first year of marriage with them.

In an effort to express our gratitude to our social network, I decided to give a speech. In the blog post, I refer to this speech and state a few of the reasons why I recited it. Here's what it said:

So. This past year has been a whirlwind for me. Not only did Dan and I get married, but I started a new job, graduated from grad school, passed my licensing exam, and we began the process to buy our building. Lots of things have been happening lately but I cannot think of a better person to be on my team than Dan. Everyone in this room knows how amazing of a person he is. I'm the luckiest.

I've got to be honest about something though. As great as he is, Dan doesn't complete me. He certainly makes life funnier. Busier. Happier. And tastier. (Dan's a chef.) But he does not complete me. And I do not complete him. Our lives are so much bigger than each other. Today illustrates that in a beautiful way.

I find it absolutely wonderful that we get to spend the last day of our first year of marriage with all of you. I've been looking forward to this moment for a long time. Because although our wedding was perfect and filled with more love than I could've ever imagined, something was missing. All of you! This was the missing piece to the puzzle of year one. It is you all who add such richness to our lives and complete us, along with the good Lord above.

Tomorrow morning, I look forward to waking up next to Mr. Robinson. I know I will feel such joy and peace. Because today has been a reminder to me that with loved ones like all of you, he and I can do this. You've got our backs. Throughout this last year, Dan and I have felt nothing but love and support from each of you. You are our community. You are the loves of our lives. We are blessed to know such amazing people.

I know it's a little odd to tell 150 people at my wedding reception, no less, that my husband does not complete me. I don't care. I stand by my statements today as much as I did back then. Here's why:

1. They're true. Dan doesn't complete me.

2. I rather enjoy challenging the things society tells us to believe, especially regarding romantic relationships. (Hopefully this book confirms that.)

3. My life is so much bigger than my marriage. My community, my faith, and my experiences complete me. My relationship with myself completes me.

4. There's a time and a place for romance, but I don't like romanticizing marriage. Our expectations of marriage are high enough as it is. (We already talked about this.)

5. I was created to tell gals that their lives are so much bigger than their romantic relationships (or lack thereof). I'll take any opportunity I can to do so. Even my wedding reception.

That's why you'll never hear me tell someone else that my husband and our marriage complete me. And I hope that in some way, you catch my drift. Whether you wholeheartedly agree with me or not, it is important that you know there is not one sole thing out there in the world that will ever complete you. So instead of searching outside, start looking within. If you look hard enough, eventually you will find what you're looking for.

It is 100% safe: If you think back to the chapter on relationship red flags, you'll remember that healthy relationships should be safe and secure spaces to express ourselves. But still, people are imperfect. You can almost bet that you will be hurt within any relationship you enter into and marriage is certainly no exception. No matter how much you trust your partner, there will likely be some area of your life that doesn't feel 100% safe to share with them. It feels odd to say, but it's true.

Think of the deepest pain you've experienced in your life. Chances are, that wrong was committed by someone you are/were really close to. The people who know us the best are the ones who have the capacity to hurt us the most. When someone hurts you, you have the option of working through the pain, forgiving the wrong, and trusting again. Marriage is filled with many of these kinds of opportunities to continually turn towards your spouse, in spite of what they may have done to hurt you.

If you strongly value safety and are a risk-averse person, a commitment like marriage might seem crazy. And in a way, I guess you're right. Promising to share your life with an imperfect person who has the capacity to hurt you deeper than anyone else on the planet is pretty darn risky. And yet, millions of people make this decision every year. Probably because the wedding industry has done a great job in getting us to think about marriage in terms of love and not in terms of risk. I, on the other hand, believe it's healthy to be mindful of both. Why? Because a healthy marriage contains both.

Consider these words from the great C.S. Lewis:

"To love at all is to be vulnerable. Love anything, and your heart will certainly be wrung and possibly be broken. If you want to make sure of keeping it intact, you must give your heart to no one, not even to an animal. Wrap it carefully round with hobbies and little luxuries; avoid all entanglements; lock it up safe in the casket or coffin of your selfishness. But in that casket—safe, dark, motionless, airless—it will change. It will not be broken; it will become unbreakable, impenetrable, irredeemable. The alternative to tragedy, or at least to the risk of tragedy, is damnation. The only place outside of Heaven where you can be perfectly safe from all the dangers and perturbations of love is Hell."

Although it may not feel completely safe, the combination of risk and love has the ability to result in true intimacy. And true intimacy is where the beauty of marriage is found. That said, don't let the risk scare you too much. Lots of scary things are worth it. It just so happens that with the right person, marriage definitely tops this list.

It is hard: Creating a life with another person and respecting their opinions is not just hard—it can be extremely hard. The hope is that the easy days will outweigh the extremely hard days, but of course, there are no guarantees of this. Some seasons of life are more difficult than others and adding a spouse to the mix means added support, yes, but also many chances for negotiation and compromise.

I have friends who are figuring out how to deal with a recent cancer diagnosis. Other friends of mine just learned that their infant is very ill. Another couple I know is caring for a father with Alzheimer's disease. All three of these couples are facing major decisions about things like medical bills and surgery options, not to mention an incredible amount of stress. I know they are grateful to have each other to lean on, but decision-making with another person can be really tough during emotionally-charged situations like these.

And there a million other things that can add strain to a marriage that have nothing to do with illness. Infidelity, debt, and natural disasters are just a handful of other life-changing events that can easily tear spouses apart. Though I'm not suggesting engaged couples attempt to plan for every awful thing that might happen to them, I do think we should never underestimate what life will throw our way or overestimate our relationship's ability to conquer the world. It takes constant maintenance over the course of time to develop a strong marriage. I'm just saying that on some days, that maintenance will feel extremely hard.

It will make you happy: Marriage can certainly enhance your happiness or add a new layer to it, but it cannot ensure your happiness. Happiness is a decision you must make on your own accord, despite what circumstances arise in your life. The honeymoon phase is just that: A phase.

Think of all the unhappily married people out there in the world or the fact that our country's divorce rate is 50%. Clearly marriage is not an automatic cure for unhappiness. Folks who expect to live "happily ever after" are highly mistaken if they are not already working towards happiness on their own. Like anything else in life, with marriage you get what you put in and sometimes even that's not enough. Making your partner or relationship responsible for your happiness is a recipe for disaster. So be very careful not to do it.

It's the beginning: A new relationship is a beginning, but it's not the beginning. Your life has already begun, so create and experience the life you want live right now, having faith that one day, Someone Special will come along and share in your amazing adventures with you. There's absolutely no need to wait for marriage to accomplish what you want to in life.

Instead, trust that the Universe has your back. Be confident that if you buy a house or move across the country to accept your dream job or adopt a furry friend, you won't be driving your life partner away, but rather, drawing them closer to you. The more you you become, the better prepared you will be to meet your Someone Special someday. It's dangerous to make decisions based on the life you wish you had, instead of the life you currently have. So make the most of the time you've been given now.

***

There are probably a thousand other myths about marriage that I've yet to learn, though I'm sure I will at some point or another. That's the thing about marriage; it doesn't shy away from teaching you the hard lessons you need to learn. It'd certainly be easier if marriage was the fairytale I planned for it to be when I was five years old, but I'll admit, I'm grateful it is not. I'm no longer hell bent on needing my husband to complete me or make me happy. I'm growing up, y'all.

Instead of letting the wedding industry spoon-feed you rainbows and butterflies, date like a woman who firmly understands the myths explained in this chapter. Then enjoy singleness like a woman who firmly understands the myths explained in this chapter, too. If you do, you'll likely be much better off whether you ever decide to get married or not. And better off is exactly what we're going for.

Questions to consider:

Why do you want to get married someday? What do you envision married life being like? In what ways can you adjust your expectations for marriage so that they are a little more realistic?

Have you heard any of these myths about marriage before? Do you agree or disagree with them? Did any of the myths surprise you or challenge you in a new way?

WHAT IF IT NEVER HAPPENS FOR ME?

"We don't reach the light by endless analysis of the dark. We reach the light by choosing the light." -Marianne Williamson

This is a question that used to run through my mind on a daily basis. Years ago I read an article that stated that 70% of black women are unmarried. This statistic absolutely scared the bejeezus out of me and for months after reading that article, I couldn't stop wondering if marriage and babies would never be in the cards for me. I was devastated.

I'm almost certain that my anxiety was amplified by the fact that so many of my friends were getting married, right around the same time I broke up with my ex-boyfriend. Wedding after wedding served as a reminder to me that not only was I nowhere close to being married, but I was also alone (I attended most of these weddings stag).

If only I had known then that my life isn't bound by statistics. Sure, statistics help us predict trends, but in life there are always outliers. There are so many things statistics cannot tell us. Statistics can't tell us about the wonderful memories single women create. They can't tell us how much joy they get from their families and friends. They can't tell us how rewarding their careers are and all the amazing places they've traveled to on their own.

Sure those things can't completely erase someone's desire to get married. No matter how full and amazing a woman's life is, she is still allowed to yearn for a life partner. But if focusing on what we don't have causes us to undervalue what we do have, there's a problem.

Instead of worrying so much about never finding someone, I wish I had focused more of my attention on the many adventures and accomplishments I wanted to experience before tying the knot or having a baby. I also wish I had focused on the things I actually enjoyed about being a single woman, instead of wishing my life away. As I've mentioned, when silver linings are hard to find, we can decide to create them ourselves. Singleness is a wonderful season of life to do just that.

This isn't to say that all the fun ends when marriage or motherhood begins. No matter what stage of life you're in, you can always set aspirations. (Carpe diem to all the wifeys and mamas out there!)

When you're not attached to a spouse or kids, however, you're able to enjoy freedom in a way many wives and mothers cannot. It can be empowering to call the shots in your own life without having to consult with someone else first. You may look to your friends and family members for guidance and support, but if you're an adult making her own money and paying most of her own bills, you probably don't have to answer to anyone about how you spend it.

Though it can be a challenge, I urge you to open your eyes to the opportunities still ahead of you, because marriage is not the only one. Chances are, you will get married someday and if you want them, you'll likely have children someday too. But before you have a spouse and kiddos vying for your attention and watching your every move, you may want to take out the time to truly enjoy the space, time, and energy you have right in front of you. Because as much as they love their children, most mothers yearn for a few moments each day where they can savor the silence and take a breather. Similarly, most wives actually look forward to a few hours away from their spouse when they have complete control of the remote.

When working with clients, I ask them to complete two different activities to help them shift their perspective a bit on singleness. First, I ask them to identify at least fifty things they like about being single. And though it is great to refer back to this list and see all the wonderful things life has to offer single women, what's most important is understanding the list-making process.

As you can imagine, some women have a really hard time identifying anything good about the single life. They feel ready to move on to the future or they're experiencing a depression that clouds their reality and makes it difficult to remain optimistic. Whatever the case may be, if this is a challenging exercise for you to complete as well, it's important to identify why.

When life is not ideal, you have two choices. You can either accept reality or resist reality. Unfortunately, if you are adamant on resisting reality, you'll not only be subjecting yourself to negativity, but you're probably subconsciously manifesting what you see around you. That's right; if you're resisting singleness, you might be perpetuating singleness. As the saying goes, what you resist, persists.

You see, though I love working with happy, independent, single women, my goal is not to make every woman head over heels in love with her singleness status. As I've said before, it's okay to desire marriage and kids and all the responsibilities they entail. In fact, I encourage my clients to openly admit that they want to be married someday. Declaring your hopes and dreams is often the first step to actualizing them.

What I do want my clients to learn, however, is how to be content with their current reality. Contentment sets us free, my friend. It removes all that pressure we feel to be different, do different, and have different. Instead, we can "let it be", distinguishing between what is within our control and what is not and spend our time focused on the former. And the best part about contentment is that we get to choose it. In spite of everything that happens to us, contentment is always an option.

After listing what they like about being single, I then ask my clients to create their Single Lady Bucket List: a list containing at least ten adventures they would like to embark on before getting married and/or having children. It's amazing to hear the things they come up with. Often times, the adventures they list are based in old childhood dreams, which is super fun to hear. No, the Bucket List cannot replace the longing to meet your Someone Special. It simply cannot.

But it sure can help you create some awesome memories until you do.

In her book, *It's Not You: 27 (Wrong) Reasons You're Single*, Sara Eckel says, "If you feel sad sometimes, it's not because you're single—it's because you're alive." I think what she's alluding to is this: Sadness is a normal human emotion, just like loneliness

and jealousy or happiness and excitement. It's important to understand that you can long for a relationship
without viewing your singleness as the root cause of
all the sadness in your life. Regardless of what season
you're in, you're going to feel sad from time to time;
that's a guarantee. So if you're not already, get used to
it.

And where it's hard to find a silver lining, create
one. (Or fifty.)

So. What if it never happens for you? Well, the
good news is that you don't have to live out that fear
today. You don't have to live out that fear tomorrow
either. Instead, you can choose contentment, remain
hopeful, refer to your list of fifty things you enjoy
about the single life (when needed), and get to work
on your bucket list. Yes, some days will be harder than
others. There may be weddings to attend on your own,
babies that elevate your baby fever, and groceries you
wish a second person could help you carry up the stairs.
Despite this, you know (or you're learning, at least)
that these moments of frustration do not have to determine your outlook on life as a whole.

In other words, you don't have to let the fear of
"what if" distract you from the potential of "what now."

Questions to consider:

What are fifty things you enjoy about your life as a single woman? Is it difficult for you to list fifty things? If so, why?

What are ten adventures you'd like to embark on as a single woman? What scares you about doing those things? What excites you about doing those things? Who in your life will be your cheerleaders as you try to accomplish what's on your Single Lady Bucket list?

WHAT TO DO WHEN YOU'RE THE LAST SINGLE GAL LEFT

"Jealousy is all the fun you think they had."

-Erica Jong

"All of my friends are getting married and I feel like I'm missing out on all the fun. HELP!"

-45% of the women who email me

Women often email me to ask me how to deal with jealousy. Being single can be tough, especially when most of your friends aren't. And boy, can I identify with this. Boy, can I ever...

I mentioned that the year I decided to end my abusive relationship was the very same year three of my closest friends got engaged. Not only was I dealing with the pain of my breakup, I was dealing with insane amounts of jealousy as well. I had done so much to make my relationship work and somehow, I still failed.

Not my friends, though. Their relationships succeeded. Why couldn't I be so lucky?

I felt absolutely miserable.

I struggled to be a good friend to these women during a time they really needed me and my jealousy ended up temporarily costing me two of these friendships. (Ironically, this only added to my loneliness.)

If you're experiencing something similar right now, breathe in and breathe out. Trust me, you can get through this and someday you won't feel so alone. Here are seven things you can do now to make sure of that.

Accept it: If all of your friends are coupling up or getting married, you need to accept it. No, it doesn't feel good to be "left behind," but singleness hardly makes you a victim, so don't act like one. I'm not going to tell you that one day soon you'll get married because I'm not God. But chances are, you probably will get married someday. And when you do, you're going to want your closest girlfriends around to support and encourage you. Accept their happiness and they will certainly return the favor.

Grieve: No one expects you to talk about fiancées, weddings, and babies 24/7 without feeling sad at times. Additionally, your friendships with these gals may be changing, and that's kind of sad too. So let yourself be sad. Good friends will make an effort to truly understand and love you through it.

Check your worth: Your friends are not finding relationships and getting married because they're

smarter, prettier, luckier, skinnier, or more successful than you. It just doesn't work that way. No, your
friends are finding relationships and getting married
because that is how life unfolded for them. And you're
single because of the way your life is unfolding. If I've
said it once, I've said it 1000 times: Your worth is not
dependent upon your relationship status. Please don't
forget that.

Make the most of it: When you are married with
three kids hanging all over you (because chances are,
that probably will happen, remember?), you'll look
back on your single days, fondly. So make the most
of them. And instead of pining after what your friends
have, fully enjoy what you have. Right now.

Own your jealousy: If you're feeling jealous,
admit it. No, you don't need to tell your married friends
about your jealousy, unless you really want to, but it's
good to tell someone. Feelings like jealousy cause us to
feel a lot of shame and the only way to break through
shame is to be open about it. Find someone to talk to.
It's not a fun emotion to feel, but jealousy points to
what we desire in our own lives. So be honest about
your jealousy, not scared of it. And if it's a part of your
truth right now, own it.

**Know the difference between feelings and
actions:** This was my biggest mistake, folks. I thought

that since I felt crappy, I was allowed to act crappy. WRONG! It's one thing to vent your frustrations to your friends, but it's quite another to treat them badly because you're upset. Find healthy ways to deal with your jealousy and sadness and don't drive all of your friends away with negativity and bitterness. No one likes hanging out with Eeyore, so if you want to throw yourself a single girl pity party, keep the invitations to yourself. (This is why you're not allowed to key your ex's car, even though Carrie said otherwise.)

Find some single friends! (At least one.): Every single gal needs a fabulous sidekick to journey through the bumps and joys of singleness. When I got stood up for a date, Nora took me out. When I went to my fifth wedding of the season with no date, Melissa texted me and kept me company during the down times. These ladies understood my life because they were going through similar experiences. Don't ditch your old friends, but try to find some new ones. Sip wine, go dancing, and have fun. Be there for each other.

As your friends couple up and marry off, it may seem like you're doomed to live a lonely life with cats. You're not (unless you want to be). This loneliness will not last forever.

So be happy for your friends. Then make some new ones. Don't give in to bitterness, and let your life flourish.

Even though it may feel like it, you're not the only single girl left.

I promise.

Questions to consider:

As your friends couple up and get married, do you feel like you're being left behind?

If so, which of your friends help you feel better about all of the changes you're observing?

YOUR INTUITION IS TRUSTWORTHY

"Your time is limited, so don't waste it living someone else's life. Don't be trapped by dogma—which is living with the results of other people's thinking. Don't let the noise of others' opinions drown out your own inner voice. And most important, have the courage to follow your heart and intuition." –Steve Jobs

When was the last time you asked a friend for her opinion on your relationship? What prompted you to ask for her opinion? Did she say what you hoped she would?

Good friends are hard to come by, so when you've found one who's willing to offer support and insight into your situation, consider yourself lucky. Goodness knows I certainly take advantage of this benefit of friendship. Heck, I talk my friends' ears off so much, they deserve trophies.

There was a time in my life, however, when I went a little overboard with my advice-seeking. My uncertainty about my relationship became the topic of every conversation. (I'm not kidding. All of them.)

One friend in particular did an excellent job in supporting me, though I think a part of this was her wanting to "fix" my problem by helping me break up with my ex. Regardless, after about two weeks of leaning on her for support, she burned out. I clearly wasn't going to break up with him, even though he was treating me very badly, and it was too painful for her to watch. I was exhausting her and eventually she had to take a step back from our friendship. This was hard for me, but necessary for her self-care.

In hindsight, I completely understand and respect her decision. At the time, however, I was devastated. Couldn't my friend see that I desperately needed her? Without her affirmation and attention, I felt lost.

The truth is, I was lost. Rather than listening to and trusting my intuition, I was expecting my friend to do that for me. But that approach was bound to fail because her desires for my life and my desires for my life were not in alignment. In fact, they were quite the opposite.

If you're not already acquainted with your intuition, I highly recommend you initiate that friendship as soon as possible. It's an important relationship that deserves your attention.

Respected

You + Your Intuition = Two Peas in a Pod

I don't care if you've made a million mistakes in the past. You're not stupid. In fact, when it comes to your life, you're an expert. The expert. Your intuition is the main reason why.

Sometimes we need the help of others. That's normal and completely okay. Find safe people who you can trust to speak truth into your life. The ones who really love you will do that well, and they'll do it often.

But never let someone speak truth into your life without first running it past your intuition. Your intuition is the gatekeeper of any and all things trying to enter your precious and worthy life.

That means blindly believing anything someone else is trying to convince you of is a big no-no.

Take this book, for example. If this all sounds like a big load of crap to you, cool. Please feel free to do the exact opposite of what I suggest, if you'd like. If any part of my message doesn't resonate with you, reject it. My feelings won't be hurt.

(Well, maybe they'll be a little hurt. But as long as your feedback is constructive, I'll be okay.)

Embrace your role as the expert of your own life. Then let that power run through your veins.

Trust your intuition. I promise you—it's a lot more trustworthy than you think it is. I believe you have exactly what you need to move forward in your life, in the best way you see fit.

I hope you believe that, too.

Questions to consider:

Do you doubt yourself a lot? Why or why not?

When was a time in your life that you just knew exactly what decision to make? How did that feel? Can you explain how you knew what you needed to do?

PART 3: LOVE, YOUR SISTERS

HOW SOME OTHER AWESOME WOMEN LEARNED TO EXPECT RESPECT

"A circle of women may be the most powerful force known to humanity. If you have one, embrace it. If you need one, seek it. If you find one, for the love of all that is good and holy, dive in. Hold on. Love it up. Get naked. Let them see you. Let them hold you. Let your reluctant tears fall. Let yourself rise fierce and love gentle. You will be changed. The very fabric of your being will be altered by this, if you allow it. Please, please allow it." –Jeanette LaBlanc

I know some of the best women in the world. Some of them are friends, others are clients, and the rest are relatives. I'm incredibly lucky. And honestly, there's no way I'd be able to write this book or do the work I do without their inspiration and support. Most of what I know about relationships is due to the interactions I have with these gals. Without them, I would not be fully myself.

That said, the stories in the pages that follow are from friends of mine. I feel honored to be able to share them with you. Heavens knows I'm not the only one who knows a thing or two about being respected while dating. Perhaps a portion of your sacred story will resonate with a portion of theirs.

Moving Forward Because My Daughters (And I!) Are Worth It

"I think the first time I began to recognize that I should have demanded respect while dating (and gotten the hell out of there if he didn't comply) was when I found out after we got married that my husband had been involved in multiple affairs since shortly after our wedding day. The hurt, shame, and broken trust that follows an affair showed me how deep the disrespect for me ran. From that time forward, I began to recognize the disrespect and abuse for what it was. It took a long time to take action though and to demand respect from my husband. By this point we had two children together and I desperately wanted our relationship to work because I didn't want to raise my girls in a broken family (or by myself). I ended up with an unwanted pregnancy (a result of the sexual abuse I endured) before I began considering what it would take to make a change. My girls are what it took for me to demand respect in my relationship with my husband. After an incident of physical abuse towards my oldest daughter, I took the steps necessary to get out of the relationship and to demand different behavior from my husband. My own childhood was riddled with incidents of abuse perpetrated by my father. I want better for my own children. My biggest motivation for demanding respect in my current relationship is my girls. I want to break the cycle of abusive relationships and disrespect that I see playing out in my siblings and I. I would like to see my girls make decisions in their dating lives that are healthy and smart and to see them find men who build them up instead of tear them down."

Staying True To Myself In A Unique Way

"As a 24-year-old virgin who has only ever had one (very short-term) boyfriend—I use that term loosely—I have learned to not only expect respect, but demand it. The first time I was rejected by a boy because I wouldn't 'put out' (at age 15, FYI), I convinced myself that there was definitely something wrong with me. When the same crap kept happening, guy after guy, year after year, I slowly began to realize that I was not in the wrong. Through college, I sat and listened to my friends tell all of their sex stories, rattling them off as easily as the alphabet, and it just hit me: You never get another first, so why waste such a special and important opportunity? So, I stopped looking for the right guy, and instead I focused on my education, my work, my responsibilities, and myself. Sure, I'm still a 24-year-old virgin, but I know that when I least expect it, some person is going to be looking for their person, and we'll both be deserving of greatness."

Learning From The Past And Sharing What I Know With Others

"When I was in my late teens to early twenties I was in a relationship that was emotionally, and at times, physically abusive. Thanks to support from family, friends and a few convenient twists of fate, I was eventually able to rid this person from my life for good. I wish I could say that from that point forward, I demanded nothing less than respect from my next relationship, but the truth is slightly more complicated. I learned a lot from that relationship, but when I left it, my self-esteem was in shambles. It took me several more years of trial, error, self-discovery, and therapy until I really was able to understand what a healthy relationship is all about and how to be in one. Heck, I'm still learning.

I spent 1.5 years dating someone who didn't respect my time, space, feelings, personal boundaries, or body. Although they claimed they loved me—they didn't—not really.

It was only later that I realized our relationship wasn't based on love or mutual respect, but on co-dependence. He broke me down emotionally, tried to change me into someone 'worthy of his love' and I believed him, trapped in a situation that wasn't unlike Stockholm syndrome.

When I left that relationship behind, I started on a journey of healing. After a lot of hard work, reflection, and heartbreak (and some mistakes along the way), I eventually arrived at my own definition of what respect means to me. Respect means that you value someone's time, feelings, and personal boundaries. It means not purposely causing someone hurt. Instead of trying to change someone, respect means that you accept them for who they are in the present moment. With that said, a huge part of 'respect' is showing yourself the same kind of love that you expect from others. Learning to love yourself, truly and deeply, is a process—one that I'm still working on. Love yourself. Know your boundaries and stick to them. The more you show yourself

Respected

the love and respect you deserve, the easier it becomes to stand up for yourself and walk away from situations and people that don't have your best interests at heart.

As a sex and dating blogger, I often get asked for relationship advice. My favorite words of advice are very much rooted in my concepts of respect:

Don't make someone a priority so you can be their option: I can't remember where I heard this saying but it stuck. Attempting to have relationships with people who are unavailable is a huge waste of energy. Same goes with putting yourself in the position of being 'the side chick'. If someone isn't willing to commit to you or let you go, they don't really respect you. Respect yourself enough to know you deserve to be in a relationship that's actually satisfying.

Put yourself first: Does the relationship you're in actually make you happy? Are your needs being met? Loving yourself means giving yourself the permission to be true to yourself, your values, and what actually makes you happy.

If something feels wrong, it is: Our intuition is way more powerful than we give it credit for. If something feels wrong or you feel like you're not being respected, you're most likely not. People will show you who they are through their actions. It's up to you to pay attention and listen.

You're not broken: Just because you've had negative experiences where you have been disrespected and had your heart crushed into a million pieces, it doesn't mean you are 'damaged'. That word implies that you can't be fixed. People heal and so will you. Negative experiences will shape who you are but you don't have to let them define you. Crappy stuff happens, but you are not this stuff.

My past experiences are what motivate me to love myself and demand respect from my relationships. Having experienced the flipside, respect is the only option."

Not Gonna Settle

"Motivation for not settling is very difficult in a world where women are often rewarded for being passive and not for being assertive in articulating what they need. It was even difficult for me. However, at the end of the day, this is my life. Not his life, not our life together, but my life. That makes the difference. No one else is responsible for my happiness.

I was recently at the crossroads of settling for a 'nice guy' who didn't even know his worth (yet I expected him to know mine) and letting it all go even though my 'clock is ticking' and I had put in several years fostering the relationship. I made a choice and I chose myself. I loved him, but I had to remember to love myself more, even though society tells me that I should be married with children by now. My quality of life counts for something and something tells me that the best is yet to come. If it's in the form of a romantic relationship—marriage and children, that'd be great! If it's in the form of self-actualization and the mani-festation of who I've become from my choice to never settle, even if it means being with myself indefinitely, well, that's great too! It hasn't been easy, but I stand by my choice. To settle in any area of life is as close to death as it gets. I choose life."

Trust Yourself

"The connection to respect and dating is this: It starts with self-respect. Honoring our intuition. Not minimizing our feelings or impressions as crazy and melodramatic. Women with anxiety issues and abuse histories are more likely to die violent deaths because we ignore primal fear as just another anxiety issue. You can't command respect and doubt yourself at the same time."

Holding On To My Standards

"Unlike most women my age, I have yet to date (unless you count that one time I met an old acquaintance for lunch in a mall food court). I am content with my current state of singleness and prefer it over casual dating for the sake of dating. I have had friends and coworkers tell me to 'just get out there', and a stranger once told me, 'Your standards are too high.' While there are certain characteristics I would like my future spouse to have (and perhaps my standards are too high), respect is one quality I am not willing to compromise. Respect is demonstrated in the way he listens to me and responds to what I have to say, how he treats me physically and emotionally, and how he views our time together. As a multicultural American, I specifically desire respect for my heritage, my family, and the unique struggles we may face as ethnic minorities. I also hope to see him show respect not just for me but for himself and others. Though I like the idea of being married someday, I would rather remain single than settle for someone who was disrespectful."

Found Love After Heartbreak

"I was married once before. I was young, truly believed I was in love, and thought he was going to be my husband forever. We were nineteen and twenty, determined to beat all of the odds against us. It only took four months for me to realize that maybe I was the only one determined to beat those odds. He was working a night shift at the time so we barely saw each other. He would come home while I was asleep and stay up until just before I had to get up for work, reasoning that he wanted to stay on his night schedule. One night after he went to work, I got on the computer to check my email and it just so happened to be signed into his. There in front of me was a world of secrets and lies. He had multiple emails from other women, all stemming from the six dating sites he had his profile on. Each profile stated he was single, never married, interested in women. Then there was a profile on a swinger site, stating that he was in a relationship and interested in adding another person for fun. I read everything through tears that streamed down my face. I didn't know what to think, I didn't know what to do. I sat on my living room floor for an hour sobbing before I started to get mad and decided to drive to his work. I confronted him and he denied it at first. But when I was able to tell him things I saw word for word he just said he was sorry, he would stop, and went back to work.

Now you might think that it was that night that I decided to demand the respect I deserved as a faithful, loving wife, but it wasn't. He did stop and he did delete the emails and the dating site accounts, but it didn't last more than six months. I caught him red handed the next time and he tried to lie to my face while his dating profile was shining boldly on the computer screen at 2 AM. He deployed right after that and was on a ship out in the middle of the ocean for six months. He got to have liberty time in the Mediterranean during the deployment and every time he sent me a picture of him in a different port I wondered if he had been unfaithful while there. (Believe it or not, it isn't uncommon for Marines to be unfaithful to their wives during their liberty time at the ports.) Right before he came home, I sent him a long email letting him know that he had one more chance. And if he couldn't prove to me that he was done with the pornography, dating sites, contacting other women, and potentially cheating on me, then I was walking away.

I would like to say that he turned himself around and we built trust and were able to walk through it together, but it never happened. As usual, he seemed okay for a while. He even had me put a password on our computer so that he couldn't get in without me. But one night while I was at work he came to see me and told me he needed to get on the computer for work and it couldn't wait until I got home. It had been almost nine months since he returned home from his deployment and he was on a regular day shift, so I decided to put my trust in him and I gave him the password. I didn't think about it until the next morning after he had gone to work to look on the computer. What he didn't know was that I had changed several settings on the computer, especially the internet, so that if there was something there, even if he had tried to delete it, I would find it. And after all that time, it wasn't just dating sites or emails, there was a real woman, a real affair, and once again I was sitting on my living room floor sobbing. Later that day when I confronted him, he became irate and backed me against the wall, then grabbed my arm so hard that I fell to floor. As he sat on my chest, pinning me on the floor, he screamed in my face and called me a bitch. The last thing he said to me as he slammed the door and left was, 'You did this.'

I finally got mad. I finally decided that enough was enough, and I finally at that moment decided that I deserved better. I stopped blaming myself for not being pretty enough, good enough in bed, or a better wife. I realized that it wasn't me, it was him. It wasn't our relationship, it was him. It wasn't anything that I could change, it was him. I tried changing myself to make him want me instead of other women and eventually had to learn that it wasn't me that had to change. In that moment, even with tears burning my cheeks and sobbing in my chest, I packed a bag and promised myself that he was done hurting me.

It was a very long road ahead and it was incredibly difficult to understand how much healing I had to do. Though he only was physically violent with me once, the emotional toll that he took on me was far worse than I realized. I fought so hard to try to maintain our marriage and I was angry with myself for fighting such a losing battle for so long. It was devastating to sign the divorce papers. The most ironic thing about it all? We signed them on what was supposed to be our wedding anniversary.

I know that I am blessed to have had my experiences and believe that they have shaped me, just as all of life's experiences do. If I had never gotten married, moved to North Carolina, and gotten divorced, I would have never met my absolute best friend and kindred spirit, Megan. I also would have never met my husband and have our beautiful girls. The Lord works in mysterious ways. He knows our hearts, He's shaped our paths, and even though we may not understand it at the time, looking back, I know in my heart that I am right where I am supposed to be."

And Still, I Am Worthy

When I was a little girl, I went to church with my brother's family. There we learned about preparing ourselves for our future spouses. The topic did not resonate with me at the time, and was too much for my adventurous spirit. I decided to take a different approach. In a soft pink journal, delicately decorated with roses and a Shetland pony on the front, I started writing love letters to my future spouse. Earlier letters describe my adventures on horseback; teenage years talk heavily on struggles with self-worth; one entry details having my sweet son at 17 years old; later years search for drive and impact. When I date, I think of these letters. I wonder: Is this man worthy of love from a woman who tried to keep her future in mind?

This story is reflective of value—both the values we infringe upon ourselves and our lives and the value we equate with our self-worth. I am eclectic and passionate; I am worthy. I am an officer in the United States Navy and yearn to deploy and serve my country; I am worthy. I am a survivor of rape; I am worthy. I am too much and never enough; I am worthy. I am not worthy for the things I do but for the faith I have and God's forgiveness. I am worthy for having a pure heart and intentions, even though I fail in execution. When one develops a sense of self-worth, based on strong values, faith, and action, one will find respect from others.

I Stood Up For Myself

"I was only married for 14 months, something that at the time seemed somewhat pitiful and probably sounded to other people that I didn't give it a fair shot. But that marriage—in fact, almost the entire relationship—was built without trust and respect. Without those two foundations to a relationship, it will, of course, crumble. It's easy to look back now at the experience and see that I didn't have the respect and trust in myself either, which is also a surefire way to make a relationship not work.

Early in our relationship, there were trust issues due to his penchant for inappropriate online messaging with women. I thought we worked through his stuff well before we were married, but as I learned just a few months after we were married, he just learned to hide things better. Those earlier indiscretions affected me in ways I didn't realize until we were in the middle of couples therapy—I let his infidelity, his jabs at my appearance and weight, and his constant going out at night instead of spending time with me, get to me in a deep way. He made me feel horrible about my life, my choices, and my family. He never laid a hand on me, but the verbal abuse, the little putdowns, they killed me in deeper ways that hurt far more than his fist ever could.

After particularly rough couples counseling session that left me hysterical in tears sitting alone in the driveway of our house as he drove to meet up with friends, I realized he didn't care about this marriage or me. He spent most of his free time with friends. I paid all the bills on my meager non-profit salary while he enjoyed financial freedom on his own paycheck that I never saw. Most of all, he spent our six months of therapy together telling me everything I was doing wrong or what he didn't like about me, instead of trying to invest the time and effort into saving our marriage. I struggled with what to do even though my family told me they would support my decision either way. I was scared of 'being divorced'—of the stigma I thought being associated with it, but most of all, knowing I had failed at the one thing I held sacred in my mind.

In July 2011, I told him I wanted a divorce. I could not quiet my inner voice telling me this was wrong any longer. I had to trust my gut. For as mean and tortured

as our marriage was, with the fights that had us screaming at each other, the decision to divorce was somewhat
amicable. I thought we could even be friends someday,
something which I laugh at now considering during the
divorce process he tried to milk me for every penny he
could, even going after the house he didn't want, just
so I didn't have it. I was a shadow of myself when I
was with him and just a bitter, angry person with no
self-respect. The minute I found out he was talking
with people online before we were engaged, I should
have dropped him, but his sweet-talking nature and my
lack of trust in myself led me to stay with him.

I stood up for myself in 2011 and I haven't looked
back. I can never shut up that voice inside me that
puts myself and my values first. When I started dating
again, I knew that any man would have to take me for
what I was: my career, my choices, and my family.
When the guy I was somewhat serious with became
judgmental about things in life that happened years
before him, I got out.

Today, I'm in a healthy, happy relationship of
a year and a half with a divorced fellow who has a
5-year-old son. Having both come from bad marriages
with disrespectful, hurtful spouses, we hold the value
of honesty, trust, and respect as crucial parts of our
love. I will never again be with a person who doesn't

accept me and all my flaws, amazingness, and craziness all together because I remember the darkness of being with someone who doesn't accept and respect me, and it's a place I can't ever go back to again."

My Faith Made All The Difference

Growing up, I was always skinny and awkward. I hated my nose and in addition to that, I was a late bloomer. I was teased constantly and male attention was far from apparent. I lived in the shadow of my friends who were swans and developed and blossomed early. Male attention was rampant for them. As for me, I longed for some male connection. It was not until my junior year of high school that I received some minimal attention from a male. Eventually, in my senior year I slightly developed and acquired a boyfriend. However, this relationship did not last long. Therefore, I had no solid grounding of what relationship should entail. I was naïve and walked around thinking idealistically about my intentions for relationships.

Entering college, I blossomed, and male attention was unrelenting. As a result, I had many offers, but the offers did not overpower my lack of self-esteem. My first serious relationship ended a year later after I found out he was unfaithful, and I was heartbroken. Eventually the relationship became violent and I would take him back, but it ended. All relationships afterward fell apart. I felt the need to always be involved with someone. I walked around thinking how a "boyfriend" was something I needed to complete me. So I always entered into relationships settling for whoever would take me.

Eventually, I met my husband and married him. We lasted about five years, only for me to find out he was alcoholic and addict. He was also emotionally abusive. I asked for a separation and eventually he decided he wanted a divorce because he was involved with someone else. Yes, he was unfaithful and left me to marry her.

After that, I decided I needed to work on myself. With therapy and with the deepening of my relationship with Christ, I realized I was loved even when only I could love myself. Developing a love for Christ and understanding my identity in Him has shown me I am worthy to be loved. Therefore, being loved by my Creator says to me that I am worthy of respect.

Even though singlehood is uncomfortable, I refuse to settle because I know who I am in Christ. This confirms that I am worthy and I deserve respect. And I do this for myself and for my daughter's sake. I choose to stay single until God ordains otherwise because I know

He has my best interest at heart. I am worth waiting for—just for who I am in Him.

Respected

"Respect is not just a song Aretha sang, but a song all little girls and grown women should be raised learning. A mantra.

When I was younger I had no boundaries and my self-image was based on whether others found me friendly, cute, sexy, or helpful. My early adult life was confused by wanting the '50's' version of happiness; a husband that worked, a home to shine, children to love.

I aimed for that and was married at 18 and divorced by 25. Two kids by 21. Remarried at 28. Beaten repeatedly before my 29th birthday. More of that until ONE DAY after many counseling sessions, my awareness grew...I needed to LOVE ME!

What!?!

Isn't that self-centered, egocentric-based arrogance?

No. A human must find their own value before it's possible to ask to be valued. I am a beautiful child of God's and that's the best kingdom to dwell in. Here and Now. Later and Forever.

I divorced the Beater/Abuser after 13 years of being made to feel small. Inside I had grown to become a much stronger version of me. One that could reply, 'Who do you think you are dealing with?' I had help on one Wednesday afternoon and a rental truck. Some co-workers and my sister came and we removed me and my belongings, leaving behind a note and 2/3 of all household possessions. I still only valued myself a third (1/3). But I got out with my life and that was everything. My only regret was putting my daughters through my hell for most of their short childhoods. They were out and of legal age by the time I left. I had no confidence I could have raised them myself. My own respect was only blooming.

Since then, I have been in a relationship with my true partner, a friend through the years. He saw me as a cute girl from high school who had weathered the storms and raised strong independent women. He believed his job on the planet was to love me so I could continue to love and care for the children and the elders. The widows. The babies. The next generation. A full circle thing.

We had a horrible year in 2012.

A major loss of respect in each of us.

Hate had grown where frustration eroded.

I left. Again. In a rented truck with my belongings.

No friends. No co-workers. Even my sister didn't know. Only my daughters knew. And my mate. He knew. He continued to love. He sought out help for his malfunctions.

A lot of counseling. Again.

But a MIRACULOUS thing happened!!!

We found our Respect, our Love, and Forgiveness. It's nothing short of amazing.

My ability to stand up for my own dignity, to respect myself enough to find out I am strong, independent of a spouse and blessed by having a true partner, lover, and friend!

Today, I am not divorced.

We reunited after one full year of separation, much more counseling, and communication towards our path and future together.

I am not afraid anymore.

I live, I love, and I am respected!"

***

Maybe one of these stories reminds you of something you've dealt with in the past or something you are experiencing right now. If so, consider how you will view your own story. Will you learn from it? Will you cope with future hardships like someone who has learned from what she is going through right now? And will you share your story for the benefit of others, so they can learn too?

I can't stress enough how incredibly important it is that you know you are not alone. Let this fact ease away any shame you feel about things you've experienced in your past. As you continue to grow, seek the support of your sisterhood—the safe women who have helped shape you into the person you are and will cheer you on and love you, no matter what you do. You need them, you really do, but don't ever forget this:

We need you too.

Questions to consider:

Who is in your sisterhood?

What lessons have they taught you?

PART 4: LOVE, YOURS TRULY

AND THEN THERE WAS FORGIVENESS

"When you forgive, you in no way change the
past—but you sure do change the future."
–Bernard Meltzer

Forgiveness: the last topic I will address in this
book. Why? Because what typically follows forgiveness is nothing short of true healing.

Most of the women I work with admit to me that
they are still holding on to anger because of an ex-partner, someone else from their past, or even themselves.
If this is the case for you, I strongly encourage you to
consider forgiveness. Carrying the pain of a breakup or
some other past hurt is tough work. Add bitterness to
the load and you'll likely end up one exhausted woman.
Negativity causes emotional atrophy.

Forgiveness opens us up to a life free of all that
negativity—the bitterness, anger, and resentment.
When one forgives another, all of the effort and energy
that was used towards being angry is now available
and up for grabs. This energy can instead be channeled
towards positive things such as growth. Rather than
focusing so much on why that person hurt you or how

they're ever going to learn right from wrong, you're finally able to focus on yourself. And since we're only ever able to control our own actions, this fact seems more than convenient.

Essentially, by forgiving someone else, you are deciding to not make them pay for the pain they caused you. You are not saying that what they did was okay, but rather, that you are choosing to move on. You are letting the Universe/God/Higher Power deal with them instead of believing that you are the one who needs to teach them a lesson. In short, you are stepping out of the way.

You are also accepting that hurt people hurt people. It's likely because of pain in their own lives that they chose to cause pain in yours. This certainly doesn't excuse their behavior, but could possibly provide an explanation for it. Reminding ourselves that pain perpetuates pain can sometimes motivate us to break the cycle of pain.

It's important to note that forgiveness is very different from reconciliation. After someone has hurt you deeply, it may not be a wise idea to let them back into your life. After a certain amount of time, you might feel better able to decide whether you'd like to reconcile with someone who's hurt you. In these situations, it's important that the person who made the mistake shows genuine regret for their actions and is committed to not hurting you in a similar way in the future. Only then can trust potentially be re-built within the relationship. In other words, when dealing with deep pain and/or betrayal, saying "I'm sorry" is simply not enough.

Even so, you don't have to have any type of relationship with a person you decide to forgive. In fact, they don't even need to know that you've decided to forgive them! Forgiveness is a decision that you can make all on your own. No one else needs to know you've chosen to forgive someone, though it can be helpful to ask for support as you relinquish control of the pain you've been caused. While reconciliation involves two individuals working together, forgiveness only involves the work and commitment of one.

Gandhi once said, "The weak can never forgive. Forgiveness is the attribute of the strong." Contrary to popular belief, forgiveness is not the "easy way out." It's hard to not demand that someone who hurt you deeply do something to make up for their transgression. For most people, it seems quite natural to hold grudges or plot revenge against someone who has hurt them. If forgiveness was a simple decision or process, I'd imagine more people would choose it as an option. The truth is, forgiveness can be a painful process in and of itself.

It is the strength of the forgiver that brings them to the other side, toward peace.

Despite how incredibly difficult it is, I will always recommend that my clients explore their lives for areas where forgiveness could be useful. I know the peace of forgiveness is worth the hard work. I've personally experienced the freedom only forgiveness can bring into our lives and want everyone to experience such a powerful release. The desire for revenge can keep us stuck and as someone who helps women move forward, it'd be unconscionable for me to not discuss forgiveness with my clients. In fact, I honestly cannot imagine full healing without it. I see a great need for more forgiveness in our society. Think of how different our world would look if more people were open to forgive.

But goodness, forgiveness is a journey. Depending on how deep your pain goes, you may need to re-commit to your decision to forgive someone else on a regular basis when you're first getting started. It can be hard when the wound feels fresh to not replay the situation in your head over and over again. This is why I do not suggest rushing forgiveness. It is important to allow yourself enough time to truly feel your feelings of pain and anger and to not deny them. As you practice trusting your intuition, you'll be able to better gauge when you might feel ready to contemplate forgiveness.

(If you find that it's taking you a considerable amount of time to move on, it might be helpful to seek the support of a professional to help you.)

***

Do you know what else is really hard? Self-forgiveness. Despite knowing that no one is perfect, we still struggle to give ourselves grace. If that is you, I urge you to forgive yourself for not knowing then what you know now. Forgive yourself for hating your body and saying bad things to it. Forgive yourself for settling for less than what you truly deserve. I mean, has staying angry at yourself ever done you any good?

Harboring resentment, especially when it's towards ourselves, is a giant roadblock to moving forward in our lives. Nobody is perfect and no one on the planet expects you to be the first. There is absolutely no way you'd be the wonderful human being you are today without all of the mistakes you've made prior to this very moment. Instead of making yourself pay for those mistakes, embrace them. Then embrace yourself. You've come a long way and you've got so much farther to go. Prepare yourself for the journey with a sloppy wet kiss from yourself.

In his book, *The Book of Forgiving: The Fourfold Path for Healing Ourselves and Our World,* Archbishop Desmond Tutu says, "With each act of forgiveness, whether small or great, we move toward wholeness." I don't know about you, but if I had to choose between wholeness and bitterness, I'm definitely going to choose the wholeness. Wholeness might require more work, but the end result is usually peace. And while world peace sure does sound nice, I'd be lying if I said I wouldn't settle for inner peace. Who knows what we could accomplish if we all just had a little more inner peace in our lives?

When I meet someone who is bitter, I'm often reminded of a rodent running on a hamster wheel. That person is usually speaking a mile a minute about how they've been wronged, which probably means their mind is racing with other thoughts as well. And yet, no matter how hard they're trying to run, I can see they are getting nowhere. If only they could get themselves off the wheel, perhaps then they could actually get some-where, if not with the other person, at least for their own sake.

Get off the wheel, my friend. Your mind does not have to race with thoughts of the past and how inade-quate you are. We're all pretty inadequate in some way or another, but that doesn't make us any less worthy of knowing the joy of moving toward true healing. Forgive yourself. No matter how long it takes for you to actually get there, it's time for you to start the journey.

It's time.

Questions to consider:

Is there anyone in your life that you feel you need to forgive? How do you feel about starting that process?

Do you need to forgive yourself? For example, are you angry with yourself about past mistakes? Do you feel guilt or shame? When you are feeling upset with yourself, what can you say to remind yourself that it's okay to make mistakes?

IN CONCLUSION

So there you have it. A few thoughts on the importance of being respected, all contained within a short self-help book. I would have never guessed in a million years that I'd write a self-help book. But I guess one of my main points throughout this book is that when we let it, life can surprise us in remarkable ways.

Over the last 150+ pages, I used the phrase "you are an adult" quite frequently. This was purposeful, for a few reasons. First, it's true. More than likely, if you're reading this, you are an adult. Second, sometimes as women, we forget that as such, our lives are meant to be lived on our terms, not anyone else's. You ought to feel empowered to make decisions that feel right for you. A key step to this is taking responsibility for your actions, while knowing who and what you are not responsible for. Lastly, I know that once you start to view yourself as an adult, others will be more likely to follow suit. And you know what? People usually respect adults.

But I'll admit, this book has very little to do with the actions of others and more with you. Whether someone else shows you respect or not is irrelevant. The true test is when you, as an adult, can identify those moments of disrespect and set up boundaries accordingly.

Will you base your self-worth off those moments or will you rest assured knowing that your worth doesn't depend on outside circumstances?

Will you appropriately care for yourself when you feel challenged or will you reach for a bag of potato chips and complain to your best friend about how life isn't fair?

Will you keep your relationship struggles to yourself or will you seek support from your trusted sisters and really listen to them, especially if a large majority of them are advising you in a similar way?

Will you replay past mistakes in your head over and over again or will you forgive yourself for not knowing then what you know now?

My hope is that after reading this book, you now know the most beneficial answers to these questions. That's not to say you'll always make the right decisions regarding your love life or other areas of your life, or that you even have to do the things I suggest in the first place. What's most important is that you know you have options.

So dare to be respected. Dare to always be respected. I can't make any promises about what will happen to your love life when you do. But maybe, just maybe, it's more than your love life that needs your full attention anyway.

THANK YOU

There's absolutely no way I could have written this book without the encouragement of so many folks. As I like to say, no woman is an island. This book is definitely proof of that. I may have written all the words, but in many ways, *Respected* is definitely a group project.

***

Thank you to my editor, Chelsea Roeser, for reading this book so many times. You just might be able to recite it by heart, I suppose.

Thank you to my designer, Natalie Robb, for creating such a wonderful cover and for doing what it took to make me really happy. You visually captured the essence of this book's content and I'm totally in awe of that.

Thank you to Miriam Fiorentino and Ernie Fraser for believing in me. You two are my safe haven and I will love you forever.

Thank you to my therapist, Michelle Snyder, for helping me through the darkest time of my life. Talking about my life with you really helped me write this book.

Thank you to girlfriends Carolyn Kuhfuss, Rachel Barsottini, Lindsey Smith, and Keely Savage. You may not realize it, but every one of our conversations gave me the confidence I needed to actually finish this.

Thank you to the eleven women who shared their stories with me and allowed me to include them in this book. I am so inspired by each of you and feel incredibly grateful to have you in my life.

Thank you to my mom for reading this book, even though some parts might have been hard to swallow. I love you for being such an amazing mother.

Thank you to my father for being the ultimate tech guru. Your intelligence blows me away. I love you for being such an amazing father.

Thank you to my husband, Dan Robinson, for letting me write about you and our life. Never once have you complained about being the subject of these writings; on the contrary, you have always encouraged me to reach for my dreams. I see it in your eyes that you believe in me and that you love me. You have taught me to so much about life, love, God, and myself. I'm a mess, but to you, I'm a beautiful mess. And you haven't given up on me yet. I love you.

RESOURCES I LIKE THAT YOU MIGHT LIKE TOO

National Domestic Violence Hotline: 1-800-799-7233 (organization)

love is respect (dot) org: http://www.loveisrespect.org (organization)

The Red Flag Campaign: http://www.theredflagcampaign.org (organization)

State Coalitions Against Domestic Violence: http://www.ovw.usdoj.gov/statedomestic.htm (list of local organizations)

101 Great Sources for Domestic Violence Prevention: http://www.socialworkdegree.net/domestic-violence-prevention (list of national organizations)

Why Does He Do That? Inside the Minds of Angry and Controlling Men by Lundy Bancroft (book)

Should I Stay or Should I Go?: A Guide to Knowing if Your Relationship Can—and Should—be Saved by Lundy Bancroft (book)

The Book of Forgiving: The Fourfold Path for Healing Ourselves and Our World by Archbishop Desmond Tutu (book)

Crazy Love by Leslie Morgan Steiner (book)

Daring Greatly by Dr. Brene Brown (book)

Make Every Man Want You: How to Be So Irresistible You'll Barely Keep from Dating Yourself! By Marie Forleo (book)

It's Not You: 27 (Wrong) Reasons You're Single by Sara Eckel (book)

ABOUT THE AUTHOR

Akirah Robinson is a licensed social worker, breakup coach, and writer who loves talking with women about their love lives. As a survivor of partner abuse, Akirah is passionate about helping women heal from heartache and teaching them how to participate in healthy relationships with others and themselves. Her work has been featured on the *Huffington Post,* Glamour.com, National Public Radio, and Australia's #1 breakfast TV show, *Sunrise.* Akirah lives in Pittsburgh, Pennsylvania with her handsome husband and enjoys playing fetch with their hyperactive hound dog, Walker. Learn more about her at **www.akirahrobinson.com.**

52519704R00100

Made in the USA
Charleston, SC
21 February 2016